TREES
FOR
SMALL
GARDENS

D0865059

GARDENERS'
POCKET PICTURE GUIDES

TREES FOR SMALL GARDENS

BRIAN DAVIS

Rodale Press, Emmaus, Pennsylvania

Designed and produced by
Breslich & Foss
Golden House
28-31 Great Pulteney Street
London W1R 3DD

Project Editor: Judy Martin
Editor: Jim Abram
Designer: Roger Daniels
Paste-up Artist: Elly King

Published in 1988 in the
United States of America by
Rodale Press, Inc
33 E. Minor St.
Emmaus, PA 18098

Text and illustrations © 1988 Brian Davis
Design © 1988 Breslich & Foss

All rights reserved. No part of this publication
may be reproduced or transmitted in any form
or by any means, electronic or mechanical,
including photocopying, recording, or any
information storage and retrieval system,
without the written permission of the
publisher.

ISBN 0-87857-744-0 Paperback

Printed and bound in Hong Kong
by Mandarin Offset

INTRODUCTION

Tree planting is a long term investment in your garden and if space is restricted it is important to select a tree, or small grouping of trees, which is precisely suited to the available space, the conditions for cultivation, and the effect you wish to achieve. A tree is the natural focal point of a small garden and should have a decorative effect – of good foliage shape and colour, attractive flowers and fruit, or unusual bark – and perhaps a particular functional value, in providing light shade for an area of the garden, for example, or screening an unattractive view. In addition its requirements should be matched to the soil type, available light and local climatic conditions. It can then become established quickly and grow to its full potential.

For this pocket guide I have selected 300 popular varieties of trees, ranging in height from 6ft (2m) to 52ft (16m) and in spread from 3ft (1m) to 32ft (10m). The smallest can be tub-grown on a patio, the largest are chosen for tall but confined habit to create a graceful and distinctive garden feature where space allows. Entries arranged alphabetically according to botanical name provide all the information you need for proper care and cultivation; a line drawing describes the overall shape of the tree so that you can see immediately if it will be suitable for the proposed location, and colour photographs display the finest features of many different varieties.

Planting a tree is a privilege and a pleasure. I hope this book will provide new opportunities for you to introduce this rewarding aspect of cultivation to even the smallest of gardens.

BRIAN DAVIS

ACER GRISEUM

PAPERBARK MAPLE
Aceraceae
Deciduous
A delightful tree, but extremely slow-growing.

Origin Introduced from China into the UK in the very early 1900s, then spread worldwide.
Use As a small ornamental bark tree for winter effect, best planted in isolation to show off its full beauty. If grouped, should be well spaced.

Acer griseum —
winter bark

Description *Flower* Small, sulphur yellow, hanging flowers in early spring. *Foliage* Olive green to grey-green, 2-3in (5-8cm) long and wide, trifoliate leaves of pendulous habit. Extremely good orange-brown autumn colouring. *Stem* Upright when young. Often loses terminal buds, but re-forms new leader shoots in spring. Branches usually borne quite low on the main stem, 3-4ft (1-1.2m) from ground level. Becomes twiggy and thin in mature growth. Its real beauty is produced on wood three years old or more, brown bark peeling away to show a golden brown underskin. *Fruit* Grey-green, aging to light brown, hanging, twin-winged seeds, often produced in large numbers on the mature tree.
Hardiness Tolerates winter temperatures down to −13°F (−25°C), but tips of new shoots vulnerable to winter damage.
Soil Requirements Most soil conditions, but extremely alkaline soils may cause chlorosis.
Sun/Shade aspect Best in full sun, but tolerates light to moderate shade. Deep shade spoils the overall shape.
Pruning None required, although removal of the lower limbs where possible enhances the trunk effect.

**Average height
and spread**
Five years
6x4ft (2x1.2m)
Ten years
13x6ft (4x2m)
*Twenty years
or at maturity*
20x10ft (6x3m)

Propagation and nursery production From seed, but very variable in its germination. Seed sown in sand-filled trays can take up to three years to germinate. Purchase container-grown up to 3ft (1m) in height. Larger plants may be found and these can be relatively safely lifted if the root ball is maintained, but will command a high price.

Problems Attains the stature of a small tree, but slow growth is characteristic. Plants 3ft (1m) are usually all that can be obtained: the tree takes time to establish itself, but is well worth waiting for.

ACER Interesting foliage varieties

NAME DEPENDENT ON VARIETY

Aceraceae
Deciduous
Interesting leaf formations in trees for all sizes of garden.

Origin Dependent on variety.

Use As ornamental trees with interesting foliage, planted singly or in groups.

Description *Flower* Green or red scale-shaped flowers in hanging clusters in early to mid spring. Details dependent on variety. *Foliage* Leaves light green, oblong to ovate or 3-5 lobed. Good autumn colour in some varieties. *Stem* Grey-green. Upright when young, becoming branching in most cases. Medium to fast rate of growth. *Fruit* Hanging small keys or winged fruits in autumn. Green or red depending on variety.

Hardiness Tolerates winter temperatures down to −13°F (−25°C).

Soil Requirements Any soil conditions.

Sun/Shade aspect Full sun to light shade, preferring full sun.

Pruning None required, but obstructive branches can be removed.

Propagation and nursery production Normally from seed, with some forms grafted. Most forms must be sought from specialist nurseries. Plant bare-rooted. Best planting heights 3-10ft (1-3m).

Problems Often only young plants are obtainable, requiring patience before the full foliage effect appears.

Varieties of interest *A. carpinifolium* (Hornbeam Maple) Shoots upright, glabrous to grey-green. Foliage oblong, 3-4in (8-10cm) long. Silky, hairy undersides when young and double-toothed edges. Flowers green, hanging on slender stalks which are 1in (3cm) long, produced in mid spring. Average height but slightly less spread. From Japan. *A. crataegifolium* (Thorn-Leaved Maple) Young shoots purple to glabrous green with white-striped veins. Forms a round-topped tree. Leaves ovate, 2-4in (5-10cm) long, with 3-5 lobes. Some yellow autumn colour. Flower clusters green-yellow, in late spring. Hanging keys or winged fruits. Slightly less than average height, but of equal spread. From Japan. *A.*

Acer saccharinum in autumn

nikoense (Nikko Maple) Hairy, grey-green shoots. Soft-textured trifoliate leaves on hairy stalks, middle leaflet oval and 3-5in (8-12cm) long, stalkless side leaflets small, ovate, with shallow toothed edges. Rich red-orange in colour in autumn. Yellow flowers hanging in threes, produced in mid spring. Keys or hanging winged fruits in autumn. One-third more than average height and spread. From Japan and China. **A. opalus** (Italian Maple) Leaves 2-4in (5-10cm) wide, 5-lobed with toothed edges, irregular, dark green to green-blue upper surfaces, paler undersides. Some yellow autumn colour. Yellow flowers in short, hanging clusters in early spring, each individual flower on a slender, glabrous, green stalk. Fruits are yellow-green keys produced in autumn. One-third more than average height and spread. From Central and Southern Europe. **A. saccharinum** syn. **A. dasycarpum** (Silver Maple) Large, palmate leaves, light grey-green when young, aging to light or mid green, silver undersides. Good yellow autumn colour. One-third more than average height and spread, a quick-growing, round-topped tree. **A. s. laciniatum** Deeply lobed, palmate leaves wih broad lacerations. Otherwise like the parent but of average height and spread. **A. s. 'Lutescens'** New spring foliage has lime green upper surfaces, silver undersides, aging to pale green in midsummer. Good autumn colours. Leaves palmate and lobed. **A. s. 'Pyramidale'** Large, palmate leaves, some dissection. Light green to grey-green with silver undersides. Good yellow autumn colour. Upright habit, reaching one-third more than average height and 13ft (4m) in width over 25 years. **A. saccharum** (Sugar Maple) Glabrous green shoots. Leaves 4-6in (10-15cm) long, wih 3-5 lobes and coarsely toothed edges. Medium to dark green with grey undersides. Hanging, green-yellow flowers presented on thin thread-like stalks up to 3in (8cm) long. Glabrous keys or winged fruits up to 2in (5cm) long in early autumn. Highly valued as shade tree for handsome form, dense foliage and fine autumn colour. A large tree, ultimately reaching up to 80ft (25m) height and 64ft (20m) spread. Used for maple syrup and sugar production in north-eastern USA. *A. s. 'Bonfire'* Good red autumn colour. *A. s. 'Globosum'* Rounded form with fine yellow autumn colour. *A. s. 'Green Mountain'* A heat-tolerant variety with leathery, dark green foliage. *A. s. 'Monumentale'* A broad columnar form with yellow-orange autumn colour. These cultivars are widely available only in their native environment. *A. triflorum* Leaves trifoliate, up to 3½in (9cm) long, ovate to oblong with limited marginal toothing. Dark green upper surfaces, light downy undersides, especially when young. Good orange-yellow autumn colour. Greenish-yellow flowers produced in threes in early spring. Keys or winged fruit 1-1¼in (3-3.5cm) long, producing a hairy central nut. Slender, branching habit. From Manchuria and Korea.

Average height and spread
Five years
13x10ft (4x3m)
Ten years
16x13ft (5x4m)
Twenty years or at maturity
23x20ft (7x6m)

ACER NEGUNDO

BOX MAPLE, ASH-LEAVED MAPLE

Aceraceae
Deciduous
An extremely useful selection of foliage-attractive Maples, ideal as small, ornamental, bushy trees. Hard pruning each spring greatly enhances the quality and variegation of the foliage.

Origin From North America.
Use As a bush or standard tree for all but the smallest gardens. Extremely attractive when planted 32ft (10m) apart in an avenue of one variety, or for an attractive hedge, bushes planted 4ft (1.2m) apart. Can be used in large containers if offered adequate annual feeding.
Description *Flower* Hanging, sulphur yellow, fluffy flowers in early spring. *Foliage* Light green, 6-8in (15-20cm) wide and long, pinnate leaves with 3-5 and sometimes up to 9 leaflets. Soft texture; slightly pendulous habit. Good yellow autumn colour. *Stem* Light to mid green, with grey-green texture when young. Upright at first, becoming dense with age. Liable to mechanical or wind breakage in exposed areas. Medium to fast rate of growth. *Fruit* Hanging, winged fruits, grey-green when young, aging to light yellow-brown. On mature trees seed is plentiful.
Hardiness Tolerates 4°F (−15°C).
Soil Requirements Does well on all soil types, unless extremely dry or poor, when it survives but may not thrive. Severely alkaline soils may cause chlorosis.
Sun/Shade aspect Tolerates full sun or light to mid shade.
Pruning None required other than removal of dead or damaged wood, but in early years can be pollarded very hard in early spring to rejuvenate larger, more attractive foliage,

especially in variegated forms, although not increasing overall height.

Propagation and nursery production *A. negundo* from seed, layering or root-stooling, but variegated forms grafted or budded except for a few found propagated by cuttings on their own roots. Can be purchased bare-rooted, container-grown or root-balled (balled-and-burlapped). For summer planting only container-grown or established containerized plants should be used. Best planting heights 3-10ft (1-3m).

Problems Any of the variegated forms may revert to producing all-green shoots, which should be removed immediately. Grafted

Acer negundo 'Elegans' **in leaf**

plants may produce suckers in early years, which should be removed.

Varieties of interest *A. n. 'Auratum'* Golden yellow foliage from spring through summer. Susceptible to leaf scorch in very hot weather. Slightly smaller growing than the parent. *A. n. var. californicum* A green-leaved form producing pink, pendulous fruits. Originating in California, it is less hardy than most and scarce in cultivation outside its native environment. *A. n. 'Elegans'* syn. *A. n. 'Elegantissimum'* Bright, yellow-edged, variegated foliage. Slightly less than average height and spread. *A. n. 'Flamingo'* Pale to rosy pink variegated leaves at tips of all new growths from late spring through early summer and often into autumn. Mature leaves variegated white. A new variety responding very well to pollarding. *A. n. 'Variegatum'* syn. *A. n. 'Argenteovariegatum'* Broad, white leaf margins but very likely to revert to green. *A. n. var. violaceum* Young shoots purple to violet and covered with white bloom. Long, hanging, dark pink flower tassels in spring. Good autumn colours. May be scarce in cultivation. Slightly less hardy.

Average height and spread
Five years
13x10ft (4x3m)
Ten years
16x13ft (5x4m)
Twenty years or at maturity
23x20ft (7x6m)

ACER PSEUDOPLATANUS 'BRILLIANTISSIMUM'

SHRIMP-LEAVED MAPLE

Aceraceae
Deciduous
An extremely attractive mop-headed tree with spring foliage colour.

Origin Of garden origin.
Use A small mop-headed tree useful for all sizes of garden. A satisfyingly round, architectural shape.
Description *Flower* Hanging clusters of green-red scale flowers in early to mid spring. *Foliage* Five-lobed, 4-7in (10-18cm) across. Lobes ovate with slightly toothed edges. New foliage deep shrimp pink, becoming flesh pink and finally green in summer. Good yellow autumn colours. *Stem* Light green, becoming green-brown. Stout, short, branching and slow-growing. *Fruit* Keys or winged fruits up to 1in (3cm) across. Light green, becoming green-brown.
Hardiness Tolerates winter temperatures down to $-13°F$ ($-25°C$).
Soil Requirements Does well on all soil types, tolerating high alkalinity.
Sun/Shade aspect Best in full sun, but tolerates very light shade.
Pruning None required.
Propagation and nursery production Grafted on to stems of *A. pseudoplatanus*. Plant bare-rooted or container-grown. Plants budded either at ground level to form large bushes or at 5ft (1.5m) or 6ft (2m) height from ground-level for standard forms.
Problems Very slow-growing when compared with other *A. pseudoplatanus* forms, but

Average height and spread
Five years
8x5ft (2.5x1.5m)
Ten years
12x8ft (3.5x2.5m)
Twenty years or at maturity
14½x12ft (4.5x3.5m)

*Acer pseudoplatanus
'Brilliantissimum'
in spring*

useful for smaller gardens. Young trees often poorly shaped due to grafting and need at least three years to develop the mop-head form. Dead and damaged twigs may be attacked by coral spot. They should be removed, cuts treated with pruning compound.
Varieties of interest *A. p. 'Prinz Handjery'* New foliage splashed shrimp pink with green base colour, aging to green, with yellow autumn colours. A large shrub or mop-headed tree, reaching 13ft (4m) in height and spread. Grafted on to stems of *A. pseudoplatanus*. Should be sought from specialist nurseries.

ACER Snake bark varieties

SNAKE-BARKED MAPLES
Aceraceae
Deciduous
Good autumn foliage colour and attractive winter colour in trunks and stems.

Origin From China or Japan, depending on variety.
Use As individual specimen trees for winter stem effect or for group planting. Interesting grown on a trunk or as lower branching shrub. Suits all but the smallest gardens.
Description *Flower* Short racemes of green to yellow-green, hanging flowers in mid spring. *Foliage* Ovate, tooth-edged leaves 2-4in (5-10cm) long and wide, normally grey-green to mid-green, producing an excellent display of orange, yellow and bronze autumn colours. *Stem* Upright when young. Depending on variety, streaked with purple or green, and white veined on two-year-old or more wood, gaining attractiveness with increasing girth. Bright red or green buds enhance the winter effect. Forms a small tree with round or spreading habit. Medium rate of growth.

Acer capillipes
in autumn

Fruit Hanging bright red or red-purple, winged fruit in autumn, green in some varieties, aging to grey-brown.

Hardiness Tolerates 4°F (−15°C).

Soil Requirements Tolerates most soil conditions, but may show decreased growth on very alkaline or dry soil.

Sun/Shade aspect Full sun to light shade.

Pruning None required other than removal of damaged or badly crossing branches. Young shoots can be pruned to control overall size. Reducing size of mature tree is extremely difficult and not advised.

Propagation and nursery production From seed, layers or grafting, depending on variety. Obtain container-grown, bare-rooted or root-balled (balled-and-burlapped). Most forms readily available from general and specialist nurseries. Best planting heights 3-10ft (1-3m).

Problems Relatively slow to mature. Often offered at no more than 3ft (1m) in height, smaller than recognized size for ornamental trees. Full snake-bark effect is achieved after 5 years.

Varieties of interest *A. capillipes* Bark purple-red to coral-red when young, aging to purple

Acer hersii −
winter branches

Average height and spread

Five years
10x5ft (3x1.5m)
Ten years
16x10ft (5x3m)
Twenty years or at maturity
23x16ft (7x5m)

with white veining. Good autumn colour. From Japan. *A. davidii* Glossy, purple-green bark with white stripes. Foliage dark green with very good autumn colours. Profuse autumn fruit production of green winged seeds, often tinged with red. Slightly less than average height and spread. From Central China. *A. d. 'Ernest Wilson'* Strong stem colour. Pink leaf petioles supporting ovate, pale green leaves. More compact than most and of slightly less than average height and spread. Somewhat difficult to find in commerical production. From the Yunnan Valley in China. *A. d. 'George Forrest'* A spreading variety with white-veined purple stems. Bright purple-red new growth in spring. Slightly less than average height but of equal spread. From the Yunnan in China. *A. grosseri* Seldom found in commercial production and may be sold as *A. grosseri var. hersii*. Light to mid green, ovate foliage changes to good autumn colour. Purple-green stems with white veining. Slightly less than average height and spread. From central China. *A. hersii* syn. *A. grosseri var. hersii* Green to grey-green, marbled bark. Ovate, mid-green foliage of good size, producing vivid autumn colours. Winged fruits produced in long racemes, light green, aging to yellow-green. From Central China. *A. pennsylvanicum* (Moosewood) Bright green young shoots, aging to grey-green with white-striped veining. Three-lobed foliage up to 6-8in (15-20cm) across; bright yellow autumn colour. Dislikes very alkaline soils. From eastern North America. *A. p. 'Erythrocladum'* Young shoots shrimp pink, aging to purple-green with white stripes. Growth production may be poor. A variey for use only as a large shrub. *A. rufinerve* Stems green-grey, almost glaucous. Mature wood has good white veining. Three-lobed leaves bright green with grey sheen, producing good red and yellow autumn colours. Two-thirds average height and spread. From Japan. *A. r. albolimbatum* New foliage in spring splashed irregularly with white variegation, maintained to midsummer. Good autumn colour. Green stems with white veining. Otherwise similar to *A. rufinerve* but scarce in commercial production and must be sought from specialist nurseries.

ALNUS INCANA

GREY ALDER

Betulaceae
Deciduous
Attractive trees for difficult, wet areas.

Origin From Europe and North America.
Use As a freestanding tree for spring catkins and interesting fruit or for mass planting to achieve a screen or windbreak.
Description *Flower* Male catkins, 2-4in (5-10cm) produced in groups of three or four. Catkins first produced in autumn, brown and scaly, opening to yellow in early spring.

Foliage Dark green upper surface with grey, downy underside. Ovate to oval, 2-4in (5-10cm) long, with tapered points and coarse tooth-edges. Some yellow autumn colour.
Stem Grey-green when young, quickly becomes purple-green and finally brown-green. Upright, fast-growing, pyramidal habit. *Fruit* Small, brown, scale-like cones produced early autumn and maintained until following spring.

Hardiness Tolerates 4°F (−15°C).

Soil Requirements Prefers moist soils but tolerates a wide range of soil types.

Sun/Shade aspect Full sun to light shade, preferring light shade.

Pruning None required but lower branches can be removed.

Propagation and nursery production From seed or layering. Can be purchased from 1½ft (50cm) up to 13ft (4m). Plant bare-rooted or container-grown. Relatively easy to find in general nurseries.

Problems None.

Varieties of interest *A. i. 'Aurea'* Golden shoots, foliage and catkins when young. Colouring decreases towards late summer, but is followed by good autumn colour. Foliage susceptible to scorch in hot summers. Requires a moist position to do well. Half average height and spread. *A. i. 'Laciniata'* Light green leaves deeply cut and lacerated. Good catkins and fruit. *A. i. 'Pendula'* Weeping branches displaying dark green, silver-backed foliage. Rarely produces a trunk. Interesting catkins and fruit. Two-thirds average height and spread.

Average height and spread
Five years
20x8ft (6x2.5m)
Ten years
39x16ft (12x5m)
Twenty years or at maturity
48x23ft (23x7m)

AMELANCHIER CANADENSIS
(Amelanchier lamarckii)

SHADBLOW SERVICEBERRY, SNOWY MESPILUS
Rosaceae
Deciduous
An attractive small tree for all sizes of garden.

**Average height
and spread**
Five years
14½x10ft (4.5x3m)
Ten years
22x16ft (6.5x5m)
*Twenty years
or at maturity*
25x20ft (7.5x6m)

Origin From North America and Canada, and now naturalized throughout most of Europe. Commonly sold in Europe and the UK as *A. lamarckii.*

Use Grown as a standard tree to make a featured specimen for small, medium or large gardens.

Description *Flower* Racemes of white flowers produced in late spring, before or just after leaves appear. *Foliage* Leaves ovate, 2-3in (5-8cm) long, light green with slight orange-red veining and shading on some soil conditions. Brilliant orange-red autumn colours. *Stem* Strong, upright when young, becoming twiggy and arching with age. Often grown as a large shrub, but readily produces a single trunk to form a small round-headed tree. Medium rate of growth. *Fruit* Small, light red fruits produced in racemes in autumn. Degree of fruiting dependent on the heat and dryness of summer.

Hardiness Tolerates winter temperatures below −13°F (−25°C).

Soil Requirements Any soil type; tolerates alkalinity and acidity.

Sun/Shade aspect Best in full sun, but tolerates quite deep shade.

Pruning None required, but any lower shoots or branches may be removed.

Propagation and nursery production From layers or by removal of a sucker from the base. On bushy plants up to 2ft (60cm) a single stem may be encouraged to develop by

*Amelanchier
canadensis* in flower

pruning. Trees pretrained up to 6-10ft (2-3m) are available. Plant bare-rooted or container-grown. Relatively easy to find in production.
Problems When grown as a standard tree is sometimes grafted on to *Crataegus oxyacantha* or *Pyrus communis*. Both these forms can be poor-rooted and produce suckers which must be removed.
Varieties of interest *A. laevis* Oval foliage producing good autumn colours. Branches more open and flowers more widely spaced, but larger individual flowers per open raceme. From eastern North America.

BETULA Coloured-stemmed varieties

BIRCH
Betulaceae
Deciduous
A fine addition to the garden for colourful winter stems: consider the location carefully to plant for best effect.

Origin From China, Korea, Japan, North America or Europe, depending on variety.
Use As individual specimen or planted in very closely grouped formations, less than 3-5ft (1-1.5m) apart to give a traditional coppice effect.
Description *Flower* Female catkins round to oval in shape, up to 1in (3cm) long and scaly-textured, small and brown when juvenile from late autumn, growing and opening with yellow stamens in early spring. *Foliage* Leaves ovate, 2-3in (5-8cm) long with toothed edges. Light grey-green when young, becoming light green with age. Good yellow autumn colour. *Stem* Light grey-green when young, aging to grey-brown; developing after 5-7 years various bark colours — orange-brown, yellow-orange, orange-grey or grey-green, depending on variety. Predominantly upright growth, medium vigour. *Fruit* Small, hanging, scaly fruits in autumn.
Hardiness Tolerant of winter temperatures below −15°F (−25°C).
Soil Requirements Tolerates a wide range of soil conditions.
Sun/Shade aspect Full sun to light shade, preferring full sun. Winter sunlight shows off coloured stems to best effect.
Pruning None required. Lower branches may be removed to enhance the appearance of trunk and stems.
Propagation and nursery production From grafting, layering or seed, dependent on variety. Plants can be obtained from 5-16ft (1.5-5m), depending on variety. Best planting heights 5-10ft (1.5-3m). Most forms must be sought from specialist nurseries, as not generally in regular production. Plant bare-rooted or container-grown.
Problems Rarely show full coloured-stem potential until 7-10 years after planting, but well worth waiting for.
Varieties of interest *B. albo-sinensis* Large attractive foliage with good autumn colour.

Betula albo-sinensis
var. septentrionalis
— trunk

**Average height
and spread**
Five years
20x5ft (6x1.5m)
Ten years
33x5ft (10x1.5m)
*Twenty years
or at maturity*
39x16ft (12x5m)

Stems acquire an orange to orange-red peeling effect of good winter value. From China. ***B. albo-sinensis var. septentrionalis*** One of the finest of all orange-stemmed birches, with bark colours orange-brown through yellow-orange to orange-grey. Old leaves give good autumn colour. Relatively scarce in commercial production. From China. ***B. ermanii*** Bark orange brown, changing with age to creamy white. Large foliage, good autumn colour. Can be damaged by late spring frosts in frost-pocket areas. From Manchuria, Korea and Japan. ***B. lenta*** (Cherry Birch) Almost black bark, non-peeling. Large foliage, good yellow autumn colour. Bark sweet and aromatic to taste and smell. From North America. ***B. lutea*** (Yellow Birch) Bark yellow to yellow-grey and of flaky composition, with bitter taste but aromatic scent. Leaves ovate to oblong, 2-4in (5-10cm) long. Good yellow autumn colour. From North America. ***B. maximowicziana*** Bark pale orange or grey with brown shoots. Large leaves up to 6in (15cm) long and 4in (10cm) wide. Two types of catkins — male 5in (12cm) long and female 2½in (6cm) long. Both produced in groups of 2-4 in long racemes. Good yellow autumn colour. The largest-leaved birch. Slightly more than average height and spread. ***B. medwediewii*** Interesting large winter terminal buds, oval and of stiff habit. Foliage ovate to round, up to 5in (12cm) long with good autumn colours, but stem colour less interesting. From Corsica.

BETULA PENDULA
(Betula alba, Betula verrucosa)

SILVER, WHITE OR COMMON BIRCH
Betulaceae
Deciduous
Delightful small trees, suitable for most gardens.

Origin From Europe through to Asia Minor.
Use As individual specimens often planted in closely grouped formations, less than 3-5ft (1-1.5m) apart to give a traditional coppice effect. Good for planting as large-scale windbreak.
Description *Flower* Round to oval female catkins, up to 1in (3cm) long and scaly in texture, brown when juvenile in late autumn, growing and opening with yellow stamens in early spring. *Foliage* Broad, ovate, ½-2in

(1-5cm) long. Light green in colour and with lobed edges. Good yellow autumn colour. *Stem* Dark purple-brown, pendulous twigs. Grey-brown young foliage becomes white-stemmed and branched with wood more than 2in (5cm) wide. Pyramidal habit, with branches pendulous towards outer ends. *Fruit* Small, hanging, scaly fruits in autumn.

Hardiness Tolerates winter temperatures below −13°F (−25°C).

Soil Requirements Tolerates a wide range of soil conditions but dislikes waterlogging.

Sun/Shade aspect Full sun to light shade, preferring full sun.

Pruning None required but removal of lower branches may enhance the appearance of the white trunk.

Propagation and nursery production From seed for basic form, or grafted for named

Betula pendula
'*Dalecarlica*' in leaf

19

Average height and spread
Five years
20x5ft (6x1.5m)
Ten years
32x10ft (10x3m)
Twenty years or at maturity
39x16ft (12x5m)

forms. Can be purchased from 1½ft (50cm) up to 16ft (5m) depending on requirements. Best planting heights 5-6ft (1.5-2m). Plant bare-rooted or container-grown. Relatively easy to find.

Problems Often required as a multi-stemmed tree, but rarely found in this form. Grouping achieves this effect. *Betulas* are relatively short-lived — 50 years being average maximum lifespan. Older trees can suddenly die for no apparent reason; this may be due to wood-boring insects.

Varieties of interest *B. p. 'Dalecarlica'* (Swedish Birch) Light green, deeply lobed foliage, lobes lanceolate with indentations. Yellow autumn colour. Upright in habit. Horizontal branches and weeping twigs. Good white stems. *B. p. 'Fastigiata'* Upright white stems, narrow columnar habit. Typical foliage, catkins and fruit. *B. p. 'Purpurea'* (Purple Leaf Birch) New foliage in spring bright purple, aging to purple-green, finally dark green. Purple catkins and fruit. Dark purple growth. Two-thirds average height and spread. Worthy of wider planting. *B. p. 'Tristis'* Typical lobed foliage with good yellow autumn colour. Upright central trunk, pendulous side branches. Extremely attractive when mature. Good white stems. *B. p. 'Youngii'* Pendulous, low, dome-shaped, spreading tree, no central leader. All branches and twigs weeping. Good white stems. Typical foliage with good yellow autumn colour. Two-thirds average height and spread.

BETULA White-stemmed varieties

BIRCH
Betulaceae
Deciduous
Splendid tall trees with beautiful bark.

Origin From north-east Asia, the Himalayas, Japan and western China, through to Europe, depending on variety.

Use As individual trees or grouped, for display of autumn colour and winter bark.

Description *Flower* Female catkins, round to oval in shape, up to 4in (10cm) long and scaly in texture; small and brown when juvenile in late autumn, growing and opening with yellow stamens in early spring. *Foliage* Leaves 2-2½in (5-6cm) long; slender, pointed, ovate or oblong. Light green with grey sheen and prominent veins. Good yellow autumn colour. *Stem* Light grey-green when young, becoming grey-brown. Finely peeling, revealing white underbark of great winter attraction. Upright pyramidal trees of medium growth rate. *Fruit* Small, hanging, scaly fruits in autumn.

Hardiness Tolerant of winter temperatures below −13°F (−25°C).

Soil Requirements Tolerant of a wide range of soil conditions; dislikes waterlogging.

Sun/Shade aspect Full sun to light shade,

preferring full sun.

Pruning No pruning other than removal of lower branches to enhance the appearance of the white trunk.

Propagation and nursery production From seed or grafts, depending on variety. Plant bare-rooted or container-grown. Trees can be purchased from 4-16ft (1.2-5m) in height. Some forms may be difficult to find and range of sizes limited; must be sought from specialist nurseries.

Problems Often required as a multi-stemmed tree, but this form is rarely found. Grouping is the way to achieve the effect. Trees are also relatively short-lived, 50 years being the average maximum lifespan. Older trees suddenly die for no apparent reason.

Varieties of interest *B. costata* Creamy-white bark with dark older bark retained, especially at leaf axils, giving a two-toned colour effect. Slightly more than average height and spread. Relatively easy to find, especially from specialist nurseries. *B. jacquemontii* Pure white stems showing well in winter light, with large areas of shaggy brown, peeling bark. Attractive autumn colours and large catkins. *B. nigra* (River Birch, Black Birch) Foliage diamond-shaped with soft green upper surfaces and glaucous undersides. Useful for planting in damp difficult areas. Extremely good on wet areas and damp ground. Native to central and eastern USA. *B. papyrifera* (Paper Birch, Canoe Birch) Large, ovate foliage, 1-4in (3-10cm) long. Bark peels in large complete sheets, revealing white underskin. Does well in moist conditions. From North America. In its native environment may reach more than average height and spread. *B. platyphylla* Very large leaves with good autumn colour. Grey-white stems. From Manchuria and Korea. *B. populifolia* (Grey Birch) Ovate light green to grey-green foliage. Attractive autumn colours. Young bark grey-white. Two-thirds average height

Average height and spread
Five years
20x5ft (6x1.5m)
Ten years
30x10ft (9x3m)
Twenty years or at maturity
39x16ft (12x5m)

and spread. Originating in North America. *B. pubescens* (White Birch) Broad ovate leaves. Yellow catkins. White bark, revealed by peeling, dark, older bark. Difficult to find. *B. utilis* Foliage ovate, coarsely tooth-edged and 2-2½in (5-6cm) long. Female yellow catkins. Bark creamy white. New shoots red-brown. Slightly less hardy. From the Himalayas.

BUDDLEIA ALTERNIFOLIA

BUDDLEIA, BUTTERFLY BUSH
Loganiaceae
Deciduous
An interesting and attractive, small weeping tree which needs training while young.

Average height and spread
Five years
12x12ft (3.5x3.5m)
Ten years
14½x14½ft (4.5x4.5m)
Twenty years or at maturity
16x16ft (5x5m)

Buddleia alternifolia **in flower**

Origin From China.
Use As a small-feature tree, planted singly or in pairs to emphasize a particular vista or walkway.
Description *Flower* Small bunches of very fragrant, small, trumpet-shaped, lilac flowers borne in early summer along graceful, arching branches. *Foliage* Grey-green, lanceolate, small leaves, giving yellow autumn colour. *Stem* Grey-green to mid green, vigorous, long and upright. Often grown as a large shrub, attaining the height of a tree after a number of years. A single stem may be encouraged and the head allowed to grow to form a small mop-headed, weeping tree. *Fruit* Brown to grey-brown seedheads in autumn and winter.
Hardiness Tolerates 4°F (−15°C).
Soil Requirements Does best in a rich, deep soil. Tolerates a wide range of other soil types, but may not attain maximum beauty.
Sun/Shade aspect Best in full sun, but tolerates light, dappled shade.

Pruning None required, other than occasional removal of very old wood.

Propagation and nursery production From softwood cuttings taken in summer or hardwood cuttings in winter. Always purchase container-grown. A tree may be formed by planting and training a young shrub. Pretrained standards can also be found. Best planting heights 2-3ft (60cm-1m).

Problems As a standard tree requires staking throughout its life to prevent physical damage by wind.

CARAGANA ARBORESCENS

PEA TREE, SIBERIAN PEASHRUB

Leguminosae
Deciduous
A group of trees offering large and small foliage forms, both being rewarding garden features.

Origin From Siberia and Manchuria.
Use As a small, low tree with attractive spring flowers, suitable for any size of garden.
Description *Flower* Small, yellow, pea-shaped

Caragana arborescens 'Pendula' in flower

flowers, borne in clusters of up to four on thin stalks mid to late spring. *Foliage* Oval to ovate, 1½-3in (4-8cm) long, produced in pairs and grouped 4-6 together; or narrow, thin, strap-like and lanceolate, very soft in texture, giving a cloud effect. Good yellow autumn colour. *Stem* Main stems spine-tipped, with secondary spines at leaf axils. Grey-green, fast-growing, slowing with age, forming a round-topped tree or large shrub. *Fruit* Small pods, 1½-2in (4-5cm) long, containing 4-6 seeds, produced in autumn.
Hardiness Tolerates winter temperatures below −13°F (−25°C).
Soil Requirements Any soil conditions; tolerates high alkalinity.
Sun/Shade aspect Best in full sun, but tolerates light shade.
Pruning None required except for training. Mature tree may resent pruning.
Propagation and nursery production From seed for parent. Named varieties from grafting on to understock of *C.arborescens*. Tree can be purchased from 3ft (1m) to 10ft (3m). *C. arborescens* is more difficult to find than its varieties. Plant bare-rooted, root-balled (balled-and-burlapped) or container-grown.

*Caragana arborescens
'Lobergii' in flower*

Problems May be late to break leaf in spring and can appear to be dead, but grows quickly once started.

Varieties of interest *C. a. 'Lorbergii'* A gem among small trees, useful for large containers. Thin, strap-like leaves give a hazy appearance, grey-green when young becoming paler with age, with good yellow autumn colour. Yellow pea-flowers produced in each leaf axil. Young trees should be pruned hard, when rapid new growth emerges to make a good head shape. This process may be repeated every 3-4 years to encourage new growth production. *C. a. 'Pendula'* A round-leaved variety, normally available on stems of 5ft (1.5m) or 8ft (2.5m), either size being suitable. Grey-green stems weep directly from

*Caragana arborescens
'Walker' in flower*

24

grafted crown to the ground and spread outwards, forming a large canopy. When young, subject to suckering, which must be removed. Quickly attains its very gnarled, weeping effect, of architectural value. *C. a. 'Walker'* Soft, strap-like foliage with yellow flowers. A small weeping tree grafted on stems of 3ft (1m), 5ft (1.5m) or 6ft (2m) in height. Growth is completely pendulous, hugging central stem. Ideal for feature planting, patio work, large rock gardens or in containers. Tolerates high winds and drought. *C. frutex* Slow-growing, spineless. Grafted on to a 5ft (1.5m) stem to make a round, tight ball of light green foliage, covered with bright yellow pea-flowers in spring. *C. maximowicziana* Normally a shrub but can be found grafted on to stems of 5ft (1.5m), forming a large, round head. Heavily armed, spiny branches. Spines white in winter. Small, grey-green foliage; dark yellow flowers in spring. From China and Tibet. *C. pygmaea* Truly a shrub, but often found grafted on to 5ft (1.5m) stems, to produce grey-green foliage in a round mop-headed effect; yellow flowers in spring. Useful for containers, rock gardens, patios and feature planting.

Average height and spread
Five years
6x6ft (2x2m)
Ten years
13x13ft (4x4m)
Twenty years or at maturity
30x20ft (9x6m)

CRATAEGUS Autumn foliage varieties

THORN
Rosaceae
Deciduous
Trees with pretty flowers and interesting autumn fruits, as well as fine foliage colours. Although deciduous, some varieties hold leaves well into autumn.

Origin Throughout the northern hemisphere.
Use A useful freestanding tree for most sizes of garden. Suitable for avenues at 32ft (10m) apart and street planting.
Description *Flower* Small white florets, ½in (1cm) across, produced in clusters 2-3in (5-8cm) wide in early summer, often with a musty scent enjoyed by bees. *Foliage* Ovate, 2-3in (5-8cm) long, light or mid green, sometimes glossy, depending on variety. Good yellow or orange autumn colour. *Stem* Medium rate of growth, forming a ball-shaped tree, very closely branched. Stems grey-green and attractive in winter. Most varieties have large thorns, normally curved and mahogany brown. *Fruit* Clusters of round, orange or crimson fruits produced in autumn; in some varieties very late to ripen.
Hardiness Tolerant of winter temperatures down to −13°F (−25°C).
Soil Requirements Most soil conditions, except very dry.
Sun/Shade aspect Full sun to medium shade, preferring light shade.
Pruning None required, but can be cut back relatively hard and any obstructing branches removed.
Propagation and nursery production From budding or grafting onto understock of *C.*

Crataegus prunifolia
in fruit

monogyna. Plant container-grown or bare-rooted. Most varieties relatively easy to find from general nurseries. Plants 6-13ft (2-4m) can be obtained. Best planting heights 6-10ft (2-3m).

Problems Slow to establish and may need two full springs to recover from transplanting. Sharp thorns can be a hazard in close garden planting.

Varieties of interest *C. 'Autumn Glory'* Excellent yellow and orange autumn colour; white flowers and red berries. Of garden origin. *C. crus-galli* (Cockspur Thorn) A flat-topped tree of more spreading habit and slightly less height. Foliage ovate to narrowly ovate, up to 3in (8cm) long, with toothed edges. Good orange-yellow autumn colours. White flowers in May followed by large clusters of long-lasting red fruits. Large thorns up to 3in (8cm) long. From North America. *C. durobrivensis* Leaves ovate with good autumn colours. White flowers followed by shining crimson berries maintained well into winter. Two-thirds average height and spread and may also be grown as a large shrub. Limited in commercial production outside its native environment of North America. *C.* × *grignonensis* Leaves ovate, up to 2½in (6cm), long, very glossy upper surface, downy grey underside. Large clusters of white flowers followed by oval to globe-shaped red fruits in autumn. Two-thirds average height and spread. Originating in France. Not readily available, but not impossible to find. *C.* × *lavallei* syn. *C. carrierei* Ovate, dark glossy green foliage with paler undersides. Good autumn colour. White flowers in clusters with dominant anthers of red and yellow. Fruits orange-red, globe-shaped, maintained well into winter. Two-thirds average height and spread. *C. mollis* Ovate leaves up to 4in (10cm) long with double-toothed edges. Light, downy grey-green at first, aging to light green. Good autumn colours. Flowers white with yellow anthers followed by large, globe-shaped, red fruits with downy texture. From North America. *C. pedicellata* (Scarlet Haw) Foliage light to mid green, slightly glossy with tooth edges. Good yellow-orange autumn colour. Numerous short thorns. White flowers in early to mid spring, followed in autumn by bunches of scarlet fruits. Two-thirds average height and spread. From north-eastern USA. *C. phaenopyrum* (Washington Thorn) Lobed, sharply tooth-edged leaves up to 2½in (6cm) long and wide. Very shiny upper surfaces, duller undersides. Good autumn colours of scarlet and orange. Clusters of white flowers followed by scarlet fruits which stay on the tree well into winter. Has an almost triangular shape. Can be diffficult to obtain. From North America. *C. pinnatifida* Interesting crimson fruits with small, dark, red-brown to black dots over their surface. Leaves light to mid green, slightly glossy with deeply cut lobes. Good orange-red autumn colour. Few thorns, in some cases not produced at all. Two-thirds average height and spread. From Northern China. Not readily available and must be sought from specialist nurseries. *C. prunifolia* Dark green, glossy foliage, round to ovate with slightly downy undersides. Round clusters of white flowers up to 2½in (6cm) across, on downy stalks, followed by rounded crimson fruits which are rarely maintained far into winter. Two-thirds average height and spread. Thought to be a cross between *C. macrantha* and *C. crus-galli*. *C. submollis* Similar to *C. mollis*, but not reaching such a great height. Plants may be intermixed in nursery production and difficult to differentiate; *C. submollis* has 10 stamens to the flower and *C. mollis* has 20.

Other varieties of good autumn-coloured *Crataegus* may be found, but the above are recommended for garden planting.

Average height and spread
Five years
13x6ft (4x2m)
Ten years
20x4ft (6x4m)
Twenty years or at maturity
26x20ft (8x6m)

CRATAEGUS OXYACANTHA

THORN, MAY, HAWTHORN

Rosaceae
Deciduous
With the other cut-leaved species and varieties listed, a group of attractive and reliable trees for late spring flowering.

Origin From Europe.
Use Ideal small round-topped trees for all types of garden. Can be severely pruned to control or shape the growth. Also useful for street planting due to the neat, tight, compact habit.
Description *Flower* Clusters of white, pink or red flowers, single or double depending on variety. Flower clusters up to 2in (5cm) across, produced in late spring. Musty scent attractive to bees. *Foliage* Basically ovate, 2in (5cm) long, very deeply lobed with 3 or 5 indentations. Grey-green with some yellow autumn tints. *Stem* Light grey-green, becoming grey-brown. Strong, upright when young,

Crataegus oxyacantha 'Paul's Scarlet' in flower

quickly branching. Armed with small, extremely sharp spines up to ½in (1cm) long. Medium rate of growth, forming a round-topped tree which spreads with age. *Fruit* Small, dull red, round to oval fruits produced in autumn containing two stone seeds, a distinctive characteristic.

Hardiness Tolerant of −13°F (−25°C).

Soil Requirements Any soil conditions, but shows signs of distress on extremely dry areas, where growth may be stunted.

Sun/Shade aspect Tolerates full sun to medium shade, preferring light shade.

Pruning None required, but responds well to being cut back hard if necessary.

Propagation and nursery production From seed for the parent; all varieties budded or

Crataegus oxyacantha 'Rosea Plena' in flower

grafted. Plant bare-rooted or container-grown. Available from 3ft (1m) up to 13ft (4m). Best planting heights 5½-6ft (1.8-2m).
Problems The sharp spines can make cultivation difficult. Suckers of understock may appear and must be removed.
Varieties of interest *C. laciniata* syn. *C. orientalis* Attractive dark grey-green, cut-leaved foliage, light grey undersides. White flowers and large dull orange-red fruits. Two-thirds average height and spread. Somewhat scarce in production. From the Orient. *C. monogyna* (Hedgerow Thorn, Singleseed Hawthorn) Single white flowers. Red, round fruits containing one stone. Foliage dark green. Rarely offered as a tree, normally used as a hedgerow plant. From Europe. *C. 'Stricta'* White flowers followed by orange-red berries. Upright growth of average height, maximum spread of 4ft (1.2m). Useful as a street tree or for planting in confined spaces. *C. × mordenensis 'Toba'* Double, creamy white flowers in the spring, followed by red berries in autumn. *C. oxyacantha 'Alba Plena'* Double white flowers in mid spring, followed by limited numbers of red berries in autumn. *C. o. 'Crimson Cloud'* Profuse single, dark pink to red flowers with yellow eyes in late spring. Good yellow-bronze-orange autumn colour. *C. o. 'Fastigiata'* Single white flowers, limited red berries. A narrow, columnar tree of average height and no more than 6ft (2m) spread. *C. o. 'Gireoudii'* New foliage on new growth mottled pink and white, aging to green. New foliage on old wood green. Bush-forming. Two-thirds average height and spread. A light annual pruning of outer extremities in early spring is recommended to encourage new variegated growth. Shy to flower, but can produce white, musty-scented flowers. Limited fruit production. Difficult to find and must be sought from specialist nurseries. *C. o. 'Paul's Scarlet'* syn. *C. o. 'Coccinea Plena'* Dark pink to red, double flowers produced late spring, early summer. Limited red berries in autumn. *C. o. 'Rosea Plena'* Double pink flowers. Produced late spring, early summer. Some limited berrying.

Average height and spread
Five years
13x4ft (4x1.2m)
Ten years
20x10ft (6x3m)
Twenty years or at maturity
20x20ft (6x6m)

CYDONIA OBLONGA

QUINCE
Rosaceae
Deciduous
Beautiful spring-flowering trees, with autumn fruits both edible and attractive.

Origin Parent from northern Iran and Turkestan; many varieties of garden origin, particularly from France.
Use As freestanding ornamental and fruiting trees. Can be grown on a stem or as large bushes. May be fan-trained on all but the most exposed walls.
Description *Flower* Saucer-shaped, delicate mother-of-pearl to light rose-pink, produced

*Cydonia oblonga
'Vranja'* in fruit

in good numbers in mid to late spring. Slightly scented. *Foliage* Leaves ovate, tooth-edged, mid to dark green with silver undersides. Good yellow autumn colour. *Stem* Upright when young, branching with age. Attractive growth formation. Branches dark brown to purple-brown, forming a round-topped large shrub or small tree. Medium to fast rate of growth. *Fruit* Medium-sized, round or pear-shaped yellow fruits, depending on variety, abundantly produced in late summer, early autumn. Used to make quince jelly.

Hardiness Tolerates −13°F (−25°C).

Soil Requirements Most soil conditions; only dislikes extremely dry or very waterlogged areas.

Sun/Shade aspect Best in full sun, to allow fruit to ripen.

Pruning None required, other than the removal of any crossing branches which may rub and form lesions. Centres may be thinned occasionally to speed up ripening of fruit. Pruning best carried out in winter.

Propagation and nursery production C. oblonga from seed; all named varieties by budding or grafting. Planted bare-rooted or container-grown. Must be sought from specialist nurseries. Best planting heights 5-8ft (1.5-2.5m).

Problems Fruiting can be a little erratic, especially after hard, late spring frosts at flowering time. Trees tend to look misshapen and irregular when young, but grow in well.

Varieties of interest *C. o. 'Meech's Prolific'* Round, squat, pear-shaped fruits produced in good quantities. Flowers not the best feature. *C. o. 'Portugal'* Small, pear-shaped fruits in profusion; a good culinary variety. Generous flower production. *C. o. 'Vranja'* Large, pear-shaped, yellow fruits. Large flowers, somewhat sparsely produced, but the tree is a fine ornamental form.

Average height and spread
Five years
10x8ft (3x2.5m)
Ten years
16x13ft (5x4m)
Twenty years or at maturity
23x20ft (7x6m)

CYTISUS × PRAECOX and CYTISUS SCOPARIUS

BROOM, WARMINSTER BROOM
Leguminosae
Deciduous
Interesting, small, mop-headed 'toy' trees for spring flowering.

Origin Of garden origin; basic forms from Europe.

Use As small trees for patios or as highlighting features in a small or medium-sized garden.

Description *Flower* Scented pea-flowers, abundantly produced and numerous colours depending on variety. *Foliage* Small, lanceolate, grey-green leaves, very sparse. *Stem* C. × praecox and C. scoparius varieties can be grafted on to a short stem of Laburnum, to form small, mop-headed to slightly pendulous standards. Stems light green to grey-green. *Fruit* Small, grey-green pea-like pods may be produced, providing winter interest.

Cytisus × praecox
in flower

Hardiness Tolerates 14°F (−10°C).

Soil Requirements Best on a neutral to acid soil. Dislikes alkaline soils, which may cause chlorosis.

Sun/Shade aspect Full sun.

Pruning None required, but small sections of year-old growth may be removed after flowering to contain shape.

Propagation and nursery production By grafting on to stems of *Laburnum vulgaris*. Purchase container-grown or root-balled (balled-and-burlapped). Relatively scarce in production as only a small number of trees are propagated each year; must be sought from specialist nurseries. Two stem sizes usually available, 3ft (1m) and 5ft (1.5m).

Problems A limited number of suckers may arise from the Laburnum understock, which should be removed when seen. Relatively

Average height and spread
Five years
6x3ft (2x1m)
Ten years
6x3ft (2x1m)
Twenty years or at maturity
6x3ft (2x1m)

short-lived plants; useful life 10-15 years.
Varieties of interest *C.* × *praecox 'Albus'* Pure white flowers. *C.* × *p. 'Allgold'* Golden yellow flowers. *C. scoparius 'Andreanus'* Crimson-red and chrome yellow flowers. *C. s. 'Burkwoodii'* Maroon and bright red flowers. *C. s. 'Windlesham Ruby'* Mahogany crimson flowers.

The above may be found grafted as mop-headed standards. Other suitable varieties may be available for garden planting.

DAVIDIA INVOLUCRATA

DOVE TREE, GHOST TREE, HANDKERCHIEF TREE
Davidiaceae
Deciduous
A beautiful flowering tree, requiring patience.

Origin From China.
Use As a spring-flowering tree for all but the smallest gardens.
Description *Flower* Small, central black flowers, flanked by two broad, ovate, pure white leaves 2½-6in (6-15cm) long, acting like flower petals to attract insects. Produced late spring, but tree will take up to 20 years from planting date to come into full flower. *Foliage* Large, deeply veined, tooth-edged leaves, mid green upper surfaces with white felted undersides. Broad to ovate, 2½-6in (6-15cm) long and 2-2½in (5-6cm) wide. Good yellow autumn colour. *Stem* Grey-green to purple-green. Strong upright shoots, over 6ft (2m) long in established plants. Branches in ascendant formation. Trees up to 20 years are pyramidal, eventually evolving a more rounded head. *Fruit* Small, round to pear-shaped fruits hanging on short stalks produced in good quantities in autumn. Green aging to green-brown.

Davidia involucrata
in flower

Hardiness Tolerates 14°F (−10°C); some terminal bud damage may occur in winter, causing stem die-back.

Soil Requirements Does best on rich, deep loam which encourages quick growth formation. Tolerates moderate alkalinity.

Sun/Shade aspect Best in light shade when young, growing into full sun with time; but tolerates medium shade to full sun.

Pruning None required once established; between young shrublet and tree stages requires some training into single central stem. Winter die-back should be removed.

Propagation and nursery production From layering. Young shrublets normally available up to 18in (45cm), often multi-stemmed. After planting a number of strong new growths appear, normally in the second spring. The best and strongest shoot is selected and trained to tree shape. It is not advisable to buy plants of more than 3ft (1m), as they may become retarded or die back. Purchase root-balled (balled-and-burlapped) or container-grown. May have to be sought from specialist nurseries, although in good years for propagation the plants are generally available.

Problems It takes a long time to train a tree and bring it to flower, but the full effect is well worth waiting for.

Varieties of interest *D. vilmoriniana* In effect identical to *D. involucrata*, often sold as the same.

Average height and spread
Five years
6x4ft (2x1.2m)
Ten years
20x12ft (6x3.5m)
Twenty years or at maturity
39x16ft (12x5m)
Continued growth can exceed
66x33ft (20x10m).

GLEDITSIA TRIACANTHOS

HONEYLOCUST
Leguminosae
Deciduous
Trees with a very wide range of habit, from tall specimens to attractive, compact ornamentals.

Origin From North America.

Use As a shade tree where space allows. Green, golden and purple varieties as small, ornamental trees for any size of garden.

Description *Flower* Green-white male flowers formed in hanging racemes 2in (5cm) long. Female flowers limited and inconspicuous. Borne in midsummer. *Foliage* Pinnate or bipinnate, up to 8in (20cm) long with up to 32 leaflets 1in (3cm) long. Light green with a

Gleditsia triacanthos in winter

glossy sheen. Good yellow autumn colour. *Stem* Light grey-green, somewhat fragile. May suffer from wind damage. Spines from 2½in (6cm) to 12in (30cm) long, produced singly or up to 7 in a bunch. Forms upright tree, crown spreading with age. Mature bark grey and deeply channelled, of architectural interest. *Fruit* Pea-shaped, grey-green pods, up to 12-18in (30-45cm) long, sword-shaped and twisted, often retained well into winter.
Hardiness Tolerates 14°F (−10°C).

Soil Requirements Best results on well-drained, deep, rich soil. Tolerates limited amount of alkalinity through to fully acid types.

Sun/Shade aspect Full sun to light shade.

Pruning None required, but shortening of previous season's growth in spring improves overall shape while young.

Propagation and nursery production From seed for the parent. Varieties grafted. Purchase container-grown 6-8ft (2-2.5m) high for best transplanting results. Should be sought from general or specialist nurseries, but some named varieties distributed through garden centres.

Problems *G. triacanthos* suffers from wind damage, losing quite large limbs, often without warning. Ornamental varieties are normally slower-growing but are small enough to resist wind damage.

Varieties of interest *G. t. 'Bujoti'* Pendulous branches covered in bright green, narrow, pinnate foliage. Good yellow autumn colour. White flowers. Reaches only one-third average height and spread. *G. t. 'Elegantissima'* Compact, only reaching one-third ultimate height and spread; can be considered as a large shrub. Interesting light green, fern-like foliage. Yellow autumn colour. *G. t. var. inermis* (Thornless Honeylocust) A small, round, mop-headed tree. Delicate light green pinnate leaves giving good autumn colour. Mature trees may produce white flowers. *G. t. 'Moraine'* Attractive light to mid green foliage. White flowers. Round habit. *G. t. 'Ruby Lace'* Foliage purple to purple-green in spring; new growth red-purple. Some yellow-bronze autumn colour. White flowers, these rarely occur. Spreading when young, eventually forming a round-topped tree. Reaches only one-third ultimate height and spread. *G. t. 'Skyline'* Attractive small light green foliage. White flowers. Upright pyramidal habit. Two-thirds average height and one-third average spread. Good for confined spaces. Difficult to find in commercial production. *G. t. 'Sunburst'* Beautiful bright golden yellow, pinnate foliage. Round-topped when young, becoming tall and upright with age. Yellow autumn colour. Two-thirds average height and spread. Responds well to pruning when young.

Average height and spread
Five years
13x6ft (4x2m)
Ten years
26x13ft (8x4m)
Twenty years or at maturity
32x26ft (10x8m)
In favourable conditions continued growth reaches 45x32ft (14x10m)

KOELREUTERIA PANICULATA

CHINESE RAIN TREE, GOLDEN RAIN TREE, PRIDE OF INDIA, CHINA TREE

Sapindaceae
Deciduous
Mid to late summer-flowering tree with interesting foliage and bark.

Koelreuteria paniculata **in flower**

Average height and spread
Five years
16x6ft (5x2m)
Ten years
26x13ft (8x4m)
Twenty years or at maturity
39x20ft (12x6m)

Origin From northern China.
Use As a small to medium height summer-flowering tree. Suitable as a solo specimen where space allows.
Description *Flower* Upright, open, terminal panicles of numerous yellow florets produced in mid to late summer. *Foliage* Light green with grey sheen. Pinnate, up to 12in (30cm) long, leaflets narrow with deeply toothed edges. Attractive light bronze when young. Good yellow autumn colour. *Stem* Light brown-green. Stiffly branched. Medium rate of growth, making a round-topped tree. *Fruit* Large, inflated, three-lobed yellow fruits in autumn.
Hardiness Tolerates 4°F (−15°C).
Soil Requirements Dislikes thin alkaline soils.
Sun/Shade aspect Best in full sun; dislikes shade.
Pruning None required.
Propagation and nursery production From seed or rooted cuttings. 'Fastigiata' is a grafted form. Plants can be transplanted root-balled (balled-and-burlapped), bare-rooted or container-grown. Plants normally supplied between 2ft (60cm) and 6ft (2m); larger plants usually scarce and not always a wise investment.
Problems Relatively short-growing and straight-stemmed specimens are extremely scarce.
Varieties of interest *K. p. apiculata* Originating in China. Less available than *K. panicula-ta*. *K. p. 'Fastigiata'* More upright habit. Average height, but a maximum of 6ft (2m) spread. Relatively scarce in commercial production.

LABURNOCYTISUS ADAMII

PINK LABURNUM
Leguminosae
Deciduous
A very attractive tree to give interest and variety.

Average height and spread
Five years
13x5ft (4x1.5m)
Ten years
20x8ft (6x2.5m)
Twenty years or at maturity
23x13ft (7x4m)

Origin A graft hybrid of *Laburnum anagy-roides* and *Cytisus purpureus*, originated in the early 1800s.
Use As a single specimen given space to show its full beauty.
Description *Flower* Individual limbs bear either racemes of yellow laburnum flowers or shorter racemes of the pink *Cytisus purpureus* flower. Some limbs may even present both flowers, one type sparsely interspersed with the other. Small areas of true *Cytisus pur-pureus* may occur in small clusters at the ends of older branches. *Foliage* Light grey-green pinnate leaves, rather untidy. On mature trees tend to be yellow and sickly. Some yellow autumn colour. *Stem* Grey-green, rub-bery texture. Upright when young, spreading with age. *Fruit* Small, poisonous pea-pods sometimes produced.
Hardiness Tolerates 4°F (−15°C).
Soil Requirements Does well on most soil conditions; tolerates heavy alkalinity or acid

Laburnocytisus adamii in flower

types. Dislikes wet conditions, when root damage may cause poor anchorage.
Sun/Shade aspect Best in full sun; tolerates light shade.
Pruning None required; may resent it.
Propagation and nursery production By grafting or budding on to *Laburnum vulgaris* understocks. Plant bare-rooted or container-grown. Best planting heights 5-10ft (1.5-3m).
Problems Root anchorage may be poor, easily dislodged in high winds. Needs staking for most of its life. Root system often feeble at time of purchase.

LABURNUM ALPINUM

ALPINE LABURNUM, SCOTCH LABURNUM

Leguminosae
Deciduous
Sometimes overlooked, but a very attractive tree, especially the dark green foliage. The weeping form can be used to great advantage as a specimen or feature plant in the smallest of gardens.

Origin From central and southern Europe.
Use As a small ornamental tree, flowering in late spring or early summer when many other flowering trees have finished. Also used as a bush or as a standard tree, and in its weeping form for tubs and containers.
Description *Flower* Pendulous racemes of fragrant, golden yellow flowers in late spring or early summer. *Foliage* Olive green, trifoliate leaves, glossy upper surfaces and paler slightly hairy undersides. *Stem* Olive green upright stems when young. Spreading with age to form a dome-shaped large bush or standard tree. *Fruit* Poisonous, hanging,

Laburnum alpinum 'Pendulum' in flower

Average height and spread
Five years
13x6ft (4x2m)
Ten years
13x10ft (4x3m)
Twenty years or at maturity
23x13ft (7x4m)

grey-green, small, pea-pod type fruits, often in great profusion, especially on mature plants.

Hardiness Tolerates −13°F (−25°C).

Soil Requirements Most soil types; likes very alkaline forms. Extremely wet conditions may lead to root-damage and unstable anchorage. Tub-grown plants need a large container and good potting soil.

Sun/Shade aspect Best in full sun, but tolerates quite deep shade.

Pruning None required; may even resent it.

Propagation and nursery production *L. alpinum* grown from seed; *'Pendulum'* form is grafted. Can be purchased bare-rooted or container-grown.

Problems Susceptible to blackfly (aphid), a winter host to this pest. Poisonous pods are dangerous to children.

Varieties of interest *L. a. 'Pendulum'* A good weeping form, reaching only about 10ft (3m) in height unless grafted. Slow-growing and weeping to the ground, with a spread of 5ft (1.5m) in time. Good display of hanging yellow flowers late spring, early summer. Grafts on a 5ft (1.5m) or 8ft (2.5m) stem can look unsightly in early years.

LABURNUM × WATERERI 'VOSSII'

GOLDEN CHAIN TREE, WATERER LABURNUM
Leguminosae
Deciduous
An interesting and well-known tree of great beauty for late spring and early summer flowering.

Origin Of garden origin.
Use As a small or medium-sized flowering tree suitable for most gardens. Can also be trained to cover archways and walkways, or as a wall climber for north or east walls.

Description *Flower* Long, hanging racemes of numerous deep yellow to golden yellow pea-flowers up to 12in (30cm) long, produced in late spring. *Foliage* Leaves trifoliate, each leaflet up to 3in (8cm) long. Grey-green to dark green, glossy upper surfaces and lighter, often hairy undersides. *Stem* Dark glossy green with a slight grey sheen. Strong, upright when young, branching and twiggy with age; finally a spreading tree of medium vigour. *Fruit* Grey-green, hanging pods containing poisonous black, pea-shaped fruits. *L. × w.* 'Vossii' produces fewer seed-pods than other Laburnums.

Hardiness Tolerates −13°F (−25°C).

Soil Requirements Any soil conditions; tolerates high alkalinity.

Sun/Shade aspect Full sun to light shade, preferring full sun.

Pruning None required; may resent it.

Propagation and nursery production By grafting. Plant bare-rooted or container-grown. Stocked by most garden centres and nurseries. Normally 6-13ft (2-4m) in height at purchase; best planting heights 8-10ft (2.5-3m).

Problems All Laburnums have poor root systems and require permanent staking. Relatively short-lived trees, showing signs of distress after 40 or more years. Poisonous fruits can be dangerous to children.

Varieties of interest *L. anagyroides* Foliage smaller and grey-tinged. Average height but slightly more spreading in habit. Flowers earlier, smaller and paler yellow than those of 'Vossii'. *L. a. 'Aureum'* Light yellow to green-yellow foliage. Not a strong tree, can be disappointing. *L. a. 'Pendulum'* A weeping form with small yellow flowers, but less handsome than *L. alpinum 'Pendulum'*.

Average height and spread
Five years
13x6ft (4x2m)
Ten years
20x10ft (6x3m)
Twenty years or at maturity
23x16ft (7x5m)

Laburnum × watereri 'Vossii' **in flower**

LIQUIDAMBAR STYRACIFLUA

SWEET GUM
Hamamelidaceae
Deciduous
Among the aristocrats of autumn-colour trees, suitable for most gardens.

Origin From eastern North America.
Use As a moderately compact, pyramidal tree, for good autumn colours and interesting architectural shape. Suitable for medium-sized and larger gardens.
Description *Flower* Small, inconspicuous, green-yellow flowers, without petals or in small catkins. Flowering variable and unreliable. *Foliage* Palmate leaves with 3 or 5 lobes, 3-6in (8-15cm) wide and 5-8in (12-20cm) long. Slightly glossy upper surfaces, downy undersides. Excellent orange-red autumn colour. *Stem* Upright pyramidal habit, branching regularly from low level. Medium rate of growth. Corky bark, grey-green. Can be trained with more main stem if required. *Fruit* Scarce and of no interest.
Hardiness Tolerates 4°F (−15°C).
Soil Requirements Does well on most soil conditions; tolerates high alkalinity. Best on moist, rich soil but dislikes waterlogging.
Sun/Shade aspect Full sun to light shade, preferring full sun. Deep shade decreases autumn colour-intensity and encourages more open habit.
Pruning None required.
Propagation and nursery production From seed, layering or grafting for named varieties. Planted root-balled (balled-and-burlapped) or container-grown. Plants normally available 2ft (60cm) to 8ft (2.5m), occasionally obtainable at 13ft (4m). Stocked in general

Liquidambar
styraciflua
in autumn

nurseries, but named varieties may have to be sought from specialist sources.

Problems Slow to establish after transplanted; can take up to three years to produce good new growth. New leaf appears very late in spring, even in early summer.

Varieties of interest *L. formosana* Very similar to *L. styraciflua*, but the bark is not corky or winged. Slightly more tender. From central and southern China. *L. f. var. monticola* Slightly larger leaves than *L. formosana*, otherwise similar. *L. styraciflua 'Aurea'* Golden yellow splashed variegation in spring, decreasing as summer approaches. Two-thirds average height and spread. *L. s. 'Lane Roberts'* Non-corky bark. Dark wine red autumn colours. Not widely grown, but can be found. *L. s. 'Variegata'* White creamy margins on grey-green leaves. Good autumn colour. Two-thirds average height and spread. *L. s. 'Worplesdon'* Corky bark. Good autumn colours.

Average height and spread
Five years
13x6ft (4x2m)
Ten years
26x13ft (8x4m)
Twenty years or at maturity
52x26ft (16x8m)

MAGNOLIA KOBUS
Large star-flowering varieties

STAR MAGNOLIA

Magnoliaceae
Deciduous
Early spring-flowering trees or large shrubs, very beautiful in bloom.

Origin From Japan.

Use As a freestanding small tree, or for the back of a large shrub border if adequate space is allowed.

Description *Flower* White, multi-petalled, fragrant flowers produced in small numbers within 10-15 years of planting, soon increasing to a display of spectacular proportions. *Foliage* Mid to dark green small, elliptic leaves, some yellow autumn colour. *Stem* Dark green to green-brown. Strong, upright, branching and spreading with age. *Fruit* Small green capsules of little interest.

Hardiness Tolerates −13°F (−25°C).

Soil Requirements Any soil type; tolerates moderate alkalinity.

Sun/Shade aspect Best in full sun, but tolerates light shade. To prevent frost damage in spring, plant away from early morning sun, to allow frosted flowers or flower buds to thaw out slowly without tissue damage.

Pruning None required, other than training as a single or multi-stemmed tree.

Propagation and nursery production From layers of semi-ripe cuttings taken in early summer. Purchase container-grown or root-balled (balled-and-burlapped). Found in garden centres and general nurseries. Obtainable from 2ft (60cm) to 3ft (1m). Larger plants occasionally available. *M. kobus* may also be found as a single-stemmed tree in specialist nurseries.

Problems Slow in coming to flower.

Varieties of interest *M. × loebneri* A cross between *M. kobus* and *M. stellata*. From an

Average height and spread
Five years
13x6ft (4x2m)
Ten years
20x13ft (6x4m)
Twenty years or at maturity
30x26ft (9x8m)

Magnolia × loebneri
'Merrill' in flower

early age produces a profusion of multi-petalled, fragrant, white flowers in early to mid spring. Of garden origin. *M. × l. 'Leonard Messel'* Fragrant, multi-petalled flowers, deep pink in bud opening to lilac pink. A cross between *M. kobus* and *M. stellata 'Rosea'*. Originating from the Nymans Gardens, Sussex, England. *M. × l. 'Merrill'* Large, white, fragrant flowers produced from an early age. Spectacular when mature. Raised in the Arnold Arboretum, Massachusetts, USA. *M. salicifolia* White, fragrant, narrow-petalled, star-shaped flowers in mid spring. Leaves, bark and wood are lemon-scented if bruised. From Japan.

MAGNOLIA × SOULANGIANA

TULIP MAGNOLIA, SAUCER MAGNOLIA

Magnoliaceae
Deciduous

Although not truly trees, these plants achieve tree-like proportions. The main form outclasses its own beautiful varieties and is highly recommended where a single specimen magnolia is required.

Origin Raised by Soulange-Bodin at Fromont, near Paris, France, in the early nineteenth century.
Use As a single or multi-stemmed small to medium feature tree.
Description *Flower* Light pink with purple shading at petal bases and centres. Produced before leaves in early spring. *Foliage* Leaves light green to grey-green, elliptic, 4-5in (10-12cm) long. Yellow autumn colour. *Stem* Grey-green becoming grey-brown. Flowerbuds large with hairy outer coating. Lower branches removed to form single or multi-stemmed tree after 15 or more years. *Fruit* May produce small green seed capsules.

Hardiness Tolerates 4°F (−15°C).

Soil Requirements Does well on heavy clay soils and most other types. Alkaline conditions will cause chlorosis.

Sun/Shade aspect Plant where there is no direct early morning sun in flowering time. Rapid thawing of flowers after late spring frosts causes browning.

Pruning Remove lower limbs to encourage single or multi-stemmed tree formation.

Propagation and nursery production From layers or semi-ripe cuttings taken in early summer. Purchase container-grown or root-balled (balled-and-burlapped). Plants normally supplied at recommended planting heights of 2ft (60cm) to 3ft (1m); plants occasionally available up to 6ft (2m). Rarely found as pretrained standard trees.

Problems Slow to flower, taking 5 years or more to produce a really good display.

Varieties of interest *M. × soulangiana 'Alba Superba'* Large, scented, pure white, erect, tulip-shaped flowers, petals flushed purple at the base. Growth upright. Average height but slightly less spread. *M. × s. 'Alexandrina'* Vigorous and upright. Free-flowering with large white flowers, purple-flushed at the base. Sometimes difficult to obtain. *M. × s. 'Amabilis'* Tulip-shaped, ivory-white flowers with a light purple flush at the base. May be difficult to obtain. *M. × s. 'Brozzonii'* Large white flowers with purple shading at the base. Late-flowering. Not readily available at garden centres and nurseries; needs seeking out. *M. × s. 'Lennei'* Leaves broad, ovate, up to 10-12in (25-30cm) long. Flowers goblet-shaped and with fleshy petals, rose-purple outside, creamy white stained purple inside. Produced mid to late spring; in some seasons a second limited flowering in autumn. Thought to be of garden origin from Lombardy, Italy. *M. × s. 'Lennei Alba'* Ivory-white, goblet-shaped flowers, held upright along the branches. Average height but slightly more

*Magnolia ×
soulangiana* **in flower**

Average height and spread

Five years
13x6ft (4x2m)
Ten years
20x13ft (6x4m)
Twenty years or at maturity
32x26ft (10x8m)

spreading. Not readily found in commercial production; needs seeking out. *M. × s. 'Picture'* Petals coloured purple outside, white inside. Flowers of erect habit. Flowering comes early in its lifespan. Leaves up to 10in (25cm) long, branches upright. Average height but with less spread. Not normally stocked by garden centres; must be sought from specialist nurseries. *M. × s. 'Rustica Rubra' ('Rubra')* Oval leaves 8in (20cm) long. Flowers cup-shaped and rosy red. A strong-growing variety, said to be a sport of *M. 'Lennei' M. × s. 'Speciosa'* White flowers with slight purple shading. Small leaves. Less than average height and spread. Not readily found in garden centres; must be sought from specialist outlets.

MALUS Fruiting varieties

FRUITING CRAB, CRAB APPLE
Rosaceae
Deciduous
Attractive, useful trees for blossom and fruit.

Malus 'Golden Hornet' **in fruit**

Origin Some varieties of natural origin, others of garden extraction.
Use As ornamental flowering trees with useful edible fruits.
Description *Flower* White, pink-tinged white or wine red, depending on variety. Flowers 1-1½in (3-4cm) across, produced singly or in multiple heads of 5-7 flowers in mid spring. *Foliage* Ovate, tooth-edged, 2in (5cm) long. Green or wine red, depending on variety. Some yellow autumn colour. *Stem* Light green to grey-green when young. Moderately upright, becoming green-brown, spreading and branching, forming a round-topped tree.

Moderate rate of growth. *Fruit* Colours from yellow, orange-red, through to purple-red. Shaped like miniature apples, 1-2in (3-5cm) across, which they are. Produced in late summer and early autumn. All edible, and also used to make jelly.

Hardiness Tolerates 4°F (−15°C).

Soil Requirements Most soil conditions; dislikes extreme waterlogging.

Sun/Shade aspect Best in full sun to very light shade to enhance ripening of fruit. Purple-leaved varieties must have full sun to maintain leaf colour.

Pruning Dead, crossing branches should be removed. To encourage fruit production the centre should be kept open to allow for ripening by sun.

Propagation and nursery production Some species forms grown from seed, but plants mainly grafted or budded on wild apple understock. Planted bare-rooted or container-grown. Normally supplied at 5½ft (1.8m) to 10ft (3m) in height. Smaller or larger plants may be obtainable, but recommended planting size is 6-10ft (2-3m). Most varieties readily available from general or specialist nurseries, also sometimes from garden centres.

Problems Liable to fungus diseases such as apple scab and apple mildew, damaging both foliage and fruit. Some stem canker may occur; remove by pruning and treat cuts with pruning compound.

Varieties of interest *M. 'Dartmouth'* White flowers followed by sizeable red-purple fruits. Green foliage. *M. 'Dolgo'* A white flowering form with yellow fruits held well into autumn. Used as a universal pollinator in orchards or for garden-grown trees. *M. 'Golden Hornet'* White flowers, followed by good crop of bright yellow fruits which may remain on the tree well into winter. Green foliage. Can be used as a universal pollinator for garden or orchard apple trees. *M. 'John Downie'* Conical fruits, 1in (3cm) long, bright orange

45

Average height and spread
Five years
13x5ft (4x1.5m)
Ten years
20x10ft (6x3m)
Twenty years or at maturity
26x20ft (8x6m)

shaded scarlet. One of the best for making jelly. Green foliage. More susceptible to apple scab and mildew than most varieties. *M. 'Professor Sprenger'* Flowers pink in bud, opening to white. Good crop of amber fruits retained until midwinter. Green foliage. Half average height and spread. *M. 'Red Sentinel'* White flowers followed by deep red fruits maintained beyond midwinter. Green foliage. *M.* × *robusta* (Siberian Crab) Two forms available, both with pink-tinged white flowers. *M.* × *r. 'Red Siberian'* Large crop of red fruits. Green foliage. *M.* × *r. 'Yellow Siberian'* Yellow fruits. Green foliage. *M. sylvestris* (Common Crab Apple) Flowers white shaded with pink. Fruits yellow-green, sometimes flushed red, 1-1½in (3-4cm) wide. Not readily available; must be sought from specialist nurseries. The parent of many ornamental crabs and the garden apple *M. 'Wintergold'* White flowers, pink in bud. Good crop of yellow fruit, retained into winter. Green foliage. *M. 'Wisley'* Strong-growing tree with limited purple-red to bronze-red flowers, with reddish shading and slight scent. Large purple-red fruits in autumn which although sparse are attractive for their size. Purple to purple-green foliage.

MALUS Green-leaved, flowering varieties

FLOWERING CRAB, CRAB, CRAB APPLE
Rosaceae
Deciduous
Very attractive and interesting, spring-flowering trees.

Origin Mostly of garden origin; a few direct species.
Use As small or medium-sized flowering trees for most sizes of garden. Best grown singly.
Description *Flower* White, pink-white or bi-coloured pink and white flowers 1½in (4cm) across, individually or in clusters of 5-7 flowers, producing a mass display. *Foliage* Green, ovate, 2in (5cm) long, tooth-edged, giving some yellow autumn colour. *Fruit* Normally green to yellow-green and of little attraction. *Stem* Purple-red to purple-green. Upright when young, quickly spreading and branching, forming a round-topped tree.
Hardiness Tolerates −13°F (−25°C).
Soil Requirements Most soil conditions; dislikes waterlogging.
Sun/Shade aspect Full sun to light shade, preferring full sun.
Pruning None required except removal of crossing and obstructing branches.
Propagation and nursery production From budding or grafting on to wild apple understock. Plant bare-rooted or container-grown. Can be purchased from 3ft (1m) up to 10ft (3m). Trees of 13-16ft (4-5m) occasionally available, but recommended planting heights 5½-8ft (1.8-2.5m).

Problems Can suffer from severe attacks of apple mildew and lesser attacks of apple scab.

Varieties of interest M. baccata White flowers up to 1½in (4cm) across in mid spring, followed by bright red, globe-shaped fruits. One-third more than average height and spread. From eastern Asia and north China. Normally sold in the form *M. baccata var. mandshurica*, which has slightly larger fruits. **M. Coronaria 'Charlottae'** Foliage ovate and coarsely toothed, up to 4in (10cm) long and 2in (5cm) wide. Semi-double, fragrant flowers borne singly or in twos or threes up to 1½in (4cm) across; attractive mother-of-pearl to mid pink colouring. Fruits large, green-yellow, not conspicuous. **M. 'Evereste'** A dwarf, mass-flowering variety. Flowers pink-white. One-third average height and spread. Not readily available, but not impossible to find. **M. floribunda** A pendulous variety, branches on mature trees reaching to ground. Can also be grown as large shrub. Flowers rose red in bud, opening to pink, finally fading to white, produced in mid to late spring in great profusion. Foliage smaller than most, ovate and deeply toothed. **M. 'Hillieri'** Somewhat weak constitution but worth consideration. Flowers semi-double, 1½in (4cm) wide, crimson-red in bud, opening to bright pink. Slightly pendulous habit. Very thin wood. **M. hupehensis** Fragrant flowers soft pink in bud, opening to white. Fruits yellow with red tints. Two-thirds average height and spread. Somewhat upright in habit. From China and Japan. **M. 'Katherine'** Semi-double flowers, pink in bud, finally white. Bright red fruits with yellow flushing. Two-thirds average height and spread with a globular head. Not readily found in production, but worth some research. **M. 'Lady Northcliffe'** Carmine-red buds opening to white with blush shading. Fruits small, yellow

Malus floribunda
in flower

Malus hupehensis in flower

and round. Two-thirds average height and spread. Not always available. *M.'Magdeburgensis'* A tree similar to a cultivated apple. Flowers deep red in bud, opening to blush-pink, finally becoming white. Fruits light green to green-yellow and unimportant. Two-thirds average height and spread. Not readily available, but not impossible to find. *M. sargentii* Foliage oblong with three lobes, up to 2½in (6cm) long. Some yellow autumn colour. Flowers pure white with greenish centres in clusters of 5 and 6; petals overlap. Fruits bright red. Very floriferous. Shrubby and reaches only one-third average height and spread, possibly more when grown as a standard tree. May be best grown as large shrub, though good effect when trained into small tree. Originating in Japan. *M. × scheideckeri* Coarsely toothed, small, elliptic to ovate leaves, sometimes with 3-5 lobes. Flowers pink to deep rose in clusters of 3-6. Growth very slender. Fruits yellow and round. A shrubby variety reaching one-third average height and spread. *M. 'Snow Cloud'* A relatively new variety of upright habit, reaching average height but less than average spread. Profuse white double flowers, opening from pink buds, in mid spring. Fruits inconspicuous. Foliage dark green with autumn tints. *M. spectabilis* Grey-green foliage susceptible to apple scab. Flowers rosy red in bud, opening to pale blush pink, up to 2in (5cm) across and borne in clusters of 6-8 in early spring. Fruits yellow and globe-shaped. From China. *M. 'Strathmore'* Light green foliage. A profusion of pale pink flowers. Round-topped. *M. toringoides* Foliage ovate to lanceolate up to 3in(8cm) long. Deeply lobed new foliage; that produced on older wood is less indented. Pastel autumn colours. Flowers light pink in bud opening to creamy-white, produced in clusters of 6-8. Fruit globe-shaped, yellow with scarlet flushing. Two-thirds average height and spread with a

Average height and spread
Five years
13x5ft (4x1.5m)
Ten years
20x10ft (6x3m)
Twenty years or at maturity
26x20ft (8x6m)

graceful, flat-headed effect. From China. **M. transitoria** Small-lobed foliage with small pink-white flowers and rounded yellow fruits. Excellent autumn colour. Two-thirds average height and spread. From north-west China. **M. trilobata** Leaves maple-shaped, deeply lobed, three-sectioned, mid to dark green with good autumn colour. White flowers, followed by infrequently produced yellow fruits. Originating in Eastern Mediterranean and north-eastern Greece. Two-third average height and spread. Scarce in production and will have to be sought from specialist nurseries. **M. 'Van Eseltine'** Flowers rose-scarlet in bud, opening to shell pink, semi-double. Small yellow fruits. Two-thirds average height and spread, slightly columnar habit.

MALUS Purple foliage varieties

PURPLE-LEAVED CRAB APPLE
Rosaceae
Deciduous
Among the loveliest of foliage and flowering trees for spring.

Origin Of garden or nursery origin.
Use As freestanding, small to medium-sized trees.
Description *Flower* Wine red to purple-red flowers, up to 1in (3cm) across, in clusters of 5-7 produced in great profusion in mid spring. *Foliage* Ovate, sometimes toothed, purple-red to purple-bronze. *Stem* Purple-red to purple-green. Upright when young, quickly spreading and branching to form a round-topped tree. Moderate rate of growth. *Fruit* Small, wine red fruits in early autumn, sometimes inconspicuous against the purple foliage.
Hardiness Tolerates 4°F (−15°C).
Soil Requirements Does well on most soils;

Malus 'Royalty'
in flower

Average height and spread
Five years
13x5ft (4x1.5m)
Ten years
20x10ft (6x3m)
Twenty years or at maturity
26x20ft (8x6m)

dislikes very poor or waterlogged types.

Sun/Shade aspect Full sun to very light shade. Deeper shade spoils foliage colour and shape of tree.

Pruning Any damaged or crossing branches should be removed in winter, also low or obstructing branches as necessary. Can be pruned back hard and rejuvenates over the next two or three seasons.

Propagation and nursery production From budding or grafting on to wild apple understock. Plant bare-rooted or container-grown. Can be purchased from 3ft (1m) up to 10ft (3m). Trees of 13-16ft (4-5m) occasionally available, but recommended planting heights 5½-8ft (1.8-2.5m).

Problems Can suffer severe attacks of apple mildew, lesser attacks of apple scab.

Varieties of interest *M. 'Eleyi'* Large red-purple flowers, followed by conical, purple-red fruits. Foliage red-purple, up to 4in (10cm) long. Initial growth somewhat weak. *M. 'Lemoinei'* An early nursery cross of merit. Purple foliage, crimson-purple flowers, bronze-purple fruits. *M. 'Liset'* Modern hybrid with good foliage and flowers, adequate dark red fruit. *M. 'Neville Copeman'* Foliage dull wine red, flowers pink-purple, fruits purple. Not as intensely coloured as some, but worth consideration. Not easy to find in commercial production. *M. 'Profusion'* An early nursery cross variety. Good purple-wine flowers, purple-red fruits and coppery-crimson spring foliage. Originally robust, but recently appears to be losing its overall vigour. *M. 'Red Glow'* Wine red flowers, large leaves and fruits. A good introduction, but not readily available. *M. 'Royalty'* Possibly the best purple-red leaf form. Large, disease-resistant, wine-coloured foliage and wine red flowers followed by large purple-red fruits. Becoming more widely available.

MALUS TSCHONOSKII

TSCHONOSKI CRAB APPLE
Rosaceae
Deciduous
One of the most spectacular autumn-tinted trees.

Origin From Japan.

Use As a moderately upright ornamental autumn-foliage tree.

Description *Flower* Rose-tinted at first, then white, 1½in (4cm) wide, produced in clusters of 4 or 6 in late spring. *Foliage* Ovate to broad, with slender point. 2-5in (5-12cm) long, grey felted undersides and grey-green uppers. Extremely good orange-red autumn colouring. *Stem* Grey-green to green-brown. Upright when young, spreading with age. Attractive red-black scaled buds in winter. Medium rate of growth. *Fruit* Small, brown-yellow fruits, globe-shaped and 1½in (4cm) wide, produced in autumn.

Hardiness Tolerates −13°F (−25°C).

Soil Requirements Most soil conditions, but

**Average height
and spread**
Five years
13x3ft (4x1m)
Ten years
26x5½ft (8x1.8m)
*Twenty years
or at maturity*
39x13ft (12x4m)

shows signs of distress on extremely poor types.

Sun/Shade aspect Full sun to light shade. Requires a sunny position to show off the full potential of its autumn colour.

Pruning None required other than removal of badly crossing branches.

Propagation and nursery production By grafting or budding. Plant bare-rooted or container-grown. Plants obtainable from 3ft (1m) up to 10ft (3m). Plants up to 16ft (5m) occasionally available, but 5½-10ft (1.8-3m) recommended as the best planting heights. Readily available from general nurseries, and sometimes garden centres.

Problems Susceptible to apple mildew and apple scab. Also very susceptible to stem canker; complete removal of diseased branches is the only solution.

MALUS Weeping forms

WEEPING CRAB APPLE

Rosaceae
Deciduous
Useful weeping trees for small gardens or limited spaces.

Origin Of garden origin.

Use As small to medium-sized weeping trees for all but the smallest gardens.

Description *Flower* Wine red or pink-tinged white, depending on variety, 1½in (4cm) across, in clusters of 5-7, mid spring. *Foliage* Wine red, aging to greenish to green-red or light green, depending on variety. Ovate, up to 2in (5cm) long, with broad-toothed edges. Limited autumn colour. *Stem* Purple-green to dark purple or green-red, aging to mid green depending on variety. Arching, becoming pendulous, forming a spreading, weeping tree of irregular branch formation. Medium rate

Malus 'Red Jade'
in fruit

**Average height
and spread**
Five years
6x5ft (2x1.5m)
Ten years
10x10ft (3x3m)
*Twenty years
or at maturity*
10x20ft (3x6m)
Overall height will
depend on initial
height of plant at
purchase.

of growth. *Fruit* Wine red or bright red fruits, depending on variety, from late summer into early autumn.
Hardiness Tolerates 4°F (−15°C).
Soil Requirements Most soil types; dislikes extremely poor soil.
Sun/Shade aspect Coloured-leaved varieties must be in full sun; any degree of shade tends to lessen colouring. Green-leaved varieties tolerate light shade.
Pruning None required, but crossing branches of straggling limbs can be removed.
Propagation and nursery production From grafting or budding on to a wild crab understock. Plant bare-rooted or container-grown. Plants normally supplied from 4ft (1.2m) to 6ft (2m).
Problems Can suffer from apple scab and apple mildew.
Varieties of interest *M. 'Echtermeyer'* Purple-green foliage, flowers and fruit. Arching branches. *M. 'Red Jade'* Bright green foliage, yellow autumn colour. Pink-tinged white flowers and bright red fruits. Slightly less than average height and spread.

MESPILUS GERMANICA

MEDLAR
Rosaceae
Deciduous
An interesting flowering and fruiting tree of architectural shape.

Origin From south-eastern Europe and Asia Minor.
Use As a freestanding ornamental tree with edible fruits.
Description *Flower* Single, 1-1½in (3-4cm) wide, white, 5-petalled, round flowers produced early summer. *Foliage* Elliptic to oblong, up to 5in (12cm) long. Grey-green with dull texture and downy undersides. Some yellow autumn colour. *Stem* Grey-green to grey-brown with some large, sparsely distributed spines. Branches upright when young, quickly arching to form a wide, round-topped tree. Ideally grown as a large shrub without central trunk. Roots can be unstable; without adequate staking uprooting can occur even to bush trees. *Fruit* Apple-shaped,

edible, brown, 1½in (4cm) wide medlar fruits produced in autumn. Each fruit has open crown effect at top.

Hardiness Tolerates 14°F (−10°C).

Soil Requirements Most soil conditions; dislikes excessive alkaline types.

Sun/Shade aspect Best in full sun for ripening of fruit, but tolerates moderate shade.

Pruning None required other than removal of crossing branches.

Propagation and nursery production From layers, seed or grafting. Plant bare-rooted, container-grown or root-balled (balled-and-burlapped). Plants normally available from 4ft (1.2m) up to 10ft (3m), but plants of 6ft (2m) recommended for best results. Young trees always deformed and irregular in shape and likely to have sparse root system. Must be sought from specialist nurseries.

Problems Poor root system means staking will be required for most of the tree's life.

Varieties of interest There are a number of named clones, but these are extremely scarce in commercial production. The basic form *M. germanica* often equals the named forms for fruit production.

Average height and spread
Five years
12x12ft (3.5x3.5m)
Ten years
14½x14½ft (4.5x4.5m)
Twenty years or at maturity
20x20ft (6x6m)

Mespilus germanica in fruit

MORUS

MULBERRY
Moraceae
Deciduous
Attractive, interesting, ornamental fruiting trees.

Origin From China, North America and western Asia, depending on variety.

Use As an architectural form of fruiting tree ideal for most sizes of garden.

Description *Flower* Very short, male or female catkins; produced in early spring, of little interest. *Foliage* Ovate, lobed or un-

53

Morus nigra in fruit

lobed, grey-green leaves. Individual branches may carry both leaf shapes. Good yellow autumn colour. The lighter green leaves of _Morus alba_ are used to feed silkworms. **Stem** Grey-green, corky, almost rubbery texture. Forms a spreading, short-trunk tree which may need to be staked for most of its life to prevent wind damage. **Fruit** Blackberry-shaped, dark red to black clusters of fruit. Edible and very juicy.

Hardiness Tolerates 14°F (−10°C).

Soil Requirements Best results on rich, moist, deep soil. Must be well drained.

Sun/Shade aspect Best in full sun to allow ripening of fruit, but tolerates light shade.

Pruning None required; may resent it.

Propagation and nursery production From hardwood cuttings taken in early winter. Purchase container-grown. Plants normally available from 2ft (60cm) up to 7ft (2.2m), occasionally as small standard trees up to 10ft (3m).

Problems Roots very fleshy and often poorly anchored. Cropping is extremely heavy in some localities and fruits fall when ripe.

Varieties of interest _M. alba_ (White Mulberry) Quick-growing. Light green-grey stems with large, ovate, light green foliage. Black fruits in autumn. One-third more than average height and spread, and slightly more tender. From China. _M. a. 'Laciniata'_ Leaves deeply cut and toothed. Good autumn colour. Fruits as parent. _M. a. 'Pendula'_ Stout, stiff, pendulous branches, grey-green stems, light green foliage. Architecturally attractive. Black fruits. Worth considering as a weeping tree for any garden. _M. nigra_ (Common or Black Mulberry) Good fruiting ability in all areas. Of reliable hardiness. From western Asia. _M. rubra_ (Red Mulberry) Fruits red to dark purple, and sweet. May exceed average height and spread by one-third or more. From North America, and not always successful as a garden tree elsewhere.

Average height and spread
Five years
12x4ft (3.5x1.2m)
Ten years
16x8ft (5x2.5m)
Twenty years or at maturity
26x16ft (8x5m)
Continued spreading over 35 years may be in excess of 32ft (10m)

PARROTIA PERSICA

PERSIAN PARROTIA
Hamamelidaceae
Deciduous
An aristocrat among autumn-foliage large shrubs and trees.

Origin From northern Persia to the Caucasus.
Use As a large multi-stemmed shrub or tree for autumn colour and winter flowering.
Description *Flower* Short clusters of red anthers, surrounded by dark brown or black hairy bracts, an attractive winter feature. Abundant flowers only on trees of more than 10-15 years. *Foliage* Ovate, up to 5in (12cm) long, with toothed edges. Dark green, turning to vivid orange, yellow and red in autumn. *Stem* Grey-green to grey-brown. Spreading and branching. Rarely produces a significant trunk. For 10-15 years may be considered a large shrub, then developing into a multi-stemmed tree. *Fruit* Small, inconspicuous nuts in autumn.
Hardiness Tolerates −13°F (−25°C).
Soil Requirements Requires neutral to acid soil for best results. Tolerates limited alkalinity, but this inhibits overall performance.
Sun/Shade aspect Full sun.
Pruning None required other than to keep within bounds.
Propagation and nursery production From seed or layers. Purchase root-balled (balled-and-burlapped) or container-grown. Normally supplied from 8in (20cm) to 3ft (1m), but can be infrequently obtained from 6-10ft (2-3m). Readily available from general nurseries or specialist outlets.
Problems Generally considered a tree, but appears as a large shrub for the first 10-15 years.
Varieties of interest *P. p. 'Pendula'* Good autumn colouring and more weeping bran-

Average height and spread
Five years
6x6ft (2x2m)
Ten years
13x13ft (4x4m)
Twenty years or at maturity
32x32ft (10x10m)

Parrotia persica
in autumn

ches than the parent. Scarce in production, but not impossible to find. ***Parrotiopsis jacquemontiana*** Previously known as *Parrotia jacquemontiana* and closely related to *P. persica*. Flowers consist of 4-6 creamy-white bracts, produced in late spring. Foliage ovate, light green, with good yellow autumn colour. Requires acid to neutral soil. From the Himalayas. Difficult to find and must be sought from specialist nurseries.

PRUNUS Almond trees

ALMOND
Rosaceae
Deciduous
Among the earliest to flower of spring-blossoming trees.

Origin From the Mediterranean to central Asia.
Use As small to medium flowering trees with the potential of a fruit crop on *P. dulcis*. Best planted singly to show off blossom effect.

Prunus × amygdalopersica in flower

Description *Flower* White or rose-pink. Single or double, depending on variety. Flowers up to 2in (5cm) across, usually borne on bare branches in late winter to early spring. *Foliage* Ovate to lanceolate, up to 6in (15cm) long, with finely toothed edges. Mid green to grey-green with red hue, particularly along veins and leaf stalks. Prominent glands at leaf bases. Limited autumn colour. *Stem* Red-green with slight grey sheen. Moderately vigorous when young, becoming branching and twiggy with age. Initially an upright tree, but quickly spreading. *Fruit* Elliptic, velvety, green with red hue. Splits and opens when ripe to show the smooth stone with pitted marks used as almond nut. *P. dulcis* is the true almond fruiting form.
Hardiness Tolerates 14°F (−10°C).
Soil Requirements Does best on well-drained soil.
Sun/Shade aspects Best in full sun to assist fruit-ripening. This is variable outside mild locations.
Pruning None required; resents it and bleeds a gummy resin from stems and trunk.
Propagation and nursery production From grafting or budding on to understocks of *P. amygdalus* or *P. persica*. Plant bare-rooted or

Average height and spread
Five years
13x5ft (4x1.5m)
Ten years
20x10ft (6x3m)
Twenty years or at maturity
23x16ft (7x5m)
56

container-grown. Normally offered from 5½ft (1.8m) to 9ft (2.8m). Larger trees not recommended. Available from general nurseries or specialist sources.

Problems Very susceptible to the virus diseases peach-leaf curl or peach-leaf blister, both extremely difficult to control. May also suffer from peach aphids. If soil preparation is inadequate the tree reacts by not prcducing new growth.

Varieties of interest *P.* × *amygdalo-persica* syn. *P. amygdalo 'Pollardii'* (Flowering Almond) A cross between a peach and an almond. Now presented by nurseries and garden centres as *P. amygdalo 'Pollardii'*. Fragrant, bright pink flowers in early spring. Fruits not edible. Originating in Australia. *P. dulcis* syn *P. amygdalus, P. communis* Pink flowers. Producing edible almond nuts and grown commercially. *P. triloba* Rose-pink double flowers. Non-fruiting. Obtainable grown on a 5-6ft (1.5-2m) standard stem to make a mop-headed tree. Or can be grown as large shrub.

PRUNUS PADUS

EUROPEAN BIRD CHERRY
Rosaceae
Deciduous
Spring-flowering trees of great beauty

Origin From northern Europe.
Use As a freestanding ornamental tree for all but the smallest gardens. Good singly or in groups. Can be used for windbreaks with spectacular spring display.
Description *Flower* Fragrant white racemes, either drooping or spreading, up to 6in (15cm) long and ½in (1cm) wide, in late spring or early summer when many other spring-flowering trees have finished. *Foliage* Dark green upper surfaces, duller hairy undersides. Oval, up to 5in (12cm) long with finely toothed edges. Some good yellow autumn tints. *Stem* Strong, upright and pyramidal when young, spreading and branching

Prunus padus var. colorata **in flower**

with age. Red-green to green-brown with attractive winter colour. Medium rate of growth. *Fruit* Small round black cherries with a bitter taste, produced irregularly on flowered stalks in late summer and autumn.
Hardiness Tolerates −13°F (−25°C).
Soil Requirements Any soil conditions.
Sun/Shade aspect Full sun to light shade.
Pruning None required.
Propagation and nursery production From seed for *P. padus*, or named varieties by grafting on to understocks of *P. padus*. Can also be budded on to *P. avium*. Plant bare-rooted or container-grown. Normally offered 5½-10ft (1.8-3m) in height; larger specimens occasionally available, but smaller trees best for planting.

Prunus padus 'Watereri' **in flower**

Problems None.

Varieties of interest *P.p. 'Albertii'* Shorter, fuller racemes of white flowers. Average spread but less height, more shrubby habit. *P. p. var. colorata* Short, somewhat irregular racemes of flowers, deep purple-pink in bud, paler when open. New foliage purple to purple-green. A beautiful sight from a distance, but loses effect at close quarters. *P. p. 'Purple Queen'* Foliage deep purple when young, aging to purple-green. Racemes of dark purple-pink flowers, good contrast with foliage. *P. p. 'Watereri'* Racemes up to 8in (20cm) long, white, fragrant; both pendulous and horizontal in formation. Good dark green foliage. Interesting winter purple stems.

Average height and spread
Five years
13x6ft (4x2m)
Ten years
26x13ft (8x4m)
Twenty years or at maturity
39x20ft (12x6m)

PRUNUS Plum trees

PURPLE-LEAVED PLUM

Rosaceae
Deciduous
Beautiful purple-leaved trees ideal for gardens of any size

Origin From western Asia and Caucasus.
Use As a small purple-leaved tree of good proportions. Can be planted in a line to form a large windbreak or screening. Good for any size of garden, due to its ability to be trimmed and trained.
Description *Flower* Masses of single or double flowers, white or pink, depending on variety, produced very early in spring on bare branches. *Foliage* Ovate, 2in (5cm) long, dark purple to purple-black, soft-textured compared with other *Prunus*. Some flame-red autumn colour. *Stem* Dark purple. Strong and upright when young, more branching and slower-growing with age, forming a round-topped tree of medium vigour. *Fruit* Small, round, dark purple to purple-black fruits in autumn.

Prunus × *blireana* **in flower**

Prunus cerasifera 'Nigra' in leaf

Hardiness Tolerates −13°F (−25°C).

Soil Requirements Any soil type, except extremely dry or poor conditions.

Sun/Shade aspect Full sun to very light shade. Deeper shade causes foliage colour to turn green.

Pruning None required, but can be clipped extensively from an early age to form a tight, formal shape.

Propagation and nursery production From hardwood cuttings taken in winter. Some varieties grafted. Available bare-rooted or container-grown. Normally offered as bushes up to 3ft (1m) or as standard trees from 5-10ft (1.5-3m). Larger trees may be available, but up to 10ft (3m) is best planting height. Relatively easy to find in general nurseries or

Prunus cerasifera 'Trailblazer' in fruit

garden centres.

Problems Young trees in nursery production often look short and stunted, requiring open ground to produce good growth and foliage.

Varieties of interest *P. americana* (American Red Plum) White flowers up to 1in (3cm) across, produced in clusters of two or five. Yellow fruits becoming very red as autumn progresses. Widely grown in the USA and Canada, not common in Europe. *P. × blireana* Double pink flowers up to 1in (3cm) across, very early in spring just before leaves emerge. Attractive purple foliage. *P. cerasifera* White flowers. Green, ovate leaves. Red or yellow round fruits in autumn. Best as large bush. *P. c. 'Atropurpurea'* syn. *P. c. 'Pissardii'* Flowers pink in bud, opening to white, and borne in good numbers before leaves appear. Purple fruits, unreliably produced. Useful as a screening tree or single specimen. *P.c. 'Nigra'* Flowers pink, single, small, borne early in spring before leaves emerge. Dark foliage and purple stems. *P. c. 'Rosea'* Salmon pink flowers, losing colour with age, boldly produced on purple stems. Rare in cultivation, but worthy of some research. *P. c. 'Trailblazer'* Masses of grey to grey-white flowers. Large purple-green leaves. Edible plums up to 1in (3cm) long in autumn. Crops can be heavy, giving the tree a pendulous habit of growth. *P. cerasus 'Rhexii'* Attractive double white flowers hanging in clusters in late spring. Foliage ovate, mid to dark green. Fruits red, aging to black, with an acid taste. May be difficult to find. *P. 'Cistena'* Not truly a tree, but shrub plants can be purchased grafted or budded on to 5ft (1.5m) high stems to form small mop-headed trees. White flowers produced on purple stems before leaves appear. Dark wine red foliage. Good autumn colour. Easily controlled by clipping. *P. spinosa* (Blackthorn) Masses of white flowers from early to mid spring. Dark green, elliptic leaves. Branches very twiggy with spines. Fruits produced as sloes. From Europe and North Africa. *P. s. 'Purpurea'* Rich purple leaves and white flowers. Forms a neat, compact large bush or small tree. Difficult to find; must be sought from specialist nurseries. Slightly less than average height and spread.

Other forms of *P. cerasifera* are available but the above are most suitable for garden planting.

Average height and spread
Five years
10x5ft (3x1.5m)
Ten years
20x10ft (6x3m)
Twenty years or at maturity
26x16ft (8x5m)

PRUNUS SERRULA (Prunus serrula tibetica)

PEELING BARK CHERRY

Rosaceae

Deciduous

Highly attractive winter trunk and branches.

Origin From western China.

Use As a small garden tree to show off attractive coloured trunk and branches in winter.

**Prunus serrula —
trunk in winter**

**Average height
and spread**
Five years
13x6ft (4x2m)
Ten years
16x10ft (5x3m)
*Twenty years
or at maturity*
23x13ft (7x4m)

Description *Flower* Small, uninteresting white flowers in mid spring. *Foliage* Ovate to lanceolate, leaves 2in (5cm) long, slightly toothed-edged. Light green, becoming darker green. *Stem* Main trunk branches show mahogany glossy surface interspersed with brown bark. Glossed area increases with age. A fine sight seen under strong winter sun. *Fruit* Small, round, black cherries.
Hardiness Tolerates −13°F (−25°C).
Soil Requirements Any soil type.
Sun/Shade aspect Full sun to light shade. Best seen in a position receiving maximum light in winter.
Pruning None required other than removal of lower branches to create maximum possible length of trunk.
Propagation and nursery production From grafting or budding. Occasionally from seed. Best container-grown but can be used bare-rooted. Trees normally available 5-10ft (1.5-3m) from specialist nurseries. Not normally stocked by garden centres.
Problems Young trees have only thin stems or trunks and do not show full potential for 5-10 years.

PRUNUS SERRULATA 'AMANOGAWA'

UPRIGHT CHERRY, LOMBARDY CHERRY
Rosaceae
Deciduous
A well-known, useful, narrow, upright flowering tree.

Origin From Japan.
Use As a tall sentinel, singly or in pairs, or making lines or avenues when planted at 16ft (5m) apart. Extremely useful for accentuating a particular area.
Description *Flower* Large clusters of semi-double, pale pink aging to off-white, slightly scented flowers abundant on the vertical branches in mid to late spring. *Foliage* Ovate to broadly lanceolate, up to 8in (20cm) long, with toothed edges. Good yellow, orange and flame autumn colours. *Stem* Grey-green to grey-brown. Upright, fastigiate habit, forming a tall, narrow pillar. *Fruit* Insignificant.
Hardiness Tolerates 4°F (−15°C).
Soil Requirements Does well on most soils, but shows signs of distress on very poor conditions.

Prunus serrulata
'Amanogawa'
in autumn

Sun/Shade aspect Best in full sun or very light shade. Deeper shade spoils the overall shape.
Pruning None required, but protruding branches can be removed, the cuts dressed with pruning compound to prevent fungus infection.
Propagation and nursery production From grafting or budding on to understocks of *P. avium*. Normally supplied bare-rooted or container-grown, from 3-10ft (1-3m). Larger trees occasionally available, but ideal planting heights are 3-6ft (1-2m). Readily available from most garden centres and general nurseries.
Problems Heavy snowfalls can open up the centre of the tree and cause branches to splay out sideways. A binding of soft string or hosepipe, which does not cut into the upright stems, holds the shape together.
Varieties of interest There are no other suitable varieties of this form. The early-flowering variety *P. × hillieri 'Spire'* is another good upright cherry.

Average height and spread
Five years
10x3ft (3x1m)
Ten years
16x5ft (5x1.5m)
Twenty years
or at maturity
20x7ft (6x2.2m)

PRUNUS SERRULATA
Large flowering Japanese Cherries

JAPANESE FLOWERING CHERRY
Rosaceae
Deciduous
Very popular, spring-flowering trees, widely planted, with a large range of planting potential.

Origin From Japan.
Use As medium to large flowering trees for spring blossom. Can also be grown as large bushes if suitable plants can be obtained for planting. Well presented in open grass areas as tall shrubs or short trees.
Description *Flower* A profusion of dark pink, white or cream, double or single flowers

**Prunus 'Kanzan'
in flower**

depending on variety, in late spring. *Foliage* Ovate to oval leaves, 3in (8cm) long with toothed edges. Light green to mid green. Yellow or orange autumn colour depending on variety. *Stem* Grey-green to grey-brown. Upright and round-topped or spreading, depending on variety. *Fruit* Insignificant.

Hardiness Tolerates temperatures down to −13°F (−25°C).

Soil Requirements Most soil conditions, but shows signs of distress on extremely poor soils.

Sun/Shade aspect Full sun to light shade.

Pruning None required other than to confine growth as necessary. Crossing branches or limbs can be removed in winter and the cuts treated with pruning compound to prevent fungus diseases.

Propagation and nursery production From budding or grafting. Normally supplied bare-rooted or container-grown from 5-10ft (1.5-3m). Larger trees occasionally available, but often slow to establish and superseded by younger trees. Most varieties readily available from garden centres and general nurseries.

Problems Some varieties, particularly *P. 'Kanzan'* can suffer from silver-leaf virus. There is no cure and affected trees must be burned to prevent further contamination.

Varieties of interest *Prunus 'Asano'* syn. *P. serrulata var. geraldiniae* Large clusters of double deep pink flowers in mid spring. Leaves light green-bronze when young, an attractive contrast with the flowers. Two-thirds average height and spread. Not readily available. *P. 'Fudanzakura'* syn. *P. serrulata var. fudanzakura* Single white flowers, pink in bud, from late winter to early spring during mild periods. Young leaves coppery-red to red-brown in spring. Difficult to find in commercial production. *P. 'Hisakura'* Large, double or semi-double, pale pink flowers. Young leaves brown-bronze in colour. A very old variety, often confused with *P. 'Kanzan'*. **P. 'Hokusai'** Clusters of semi-double, pale pink flowers in mid spring. A round-topped tree with wide-spreading branches. **P. 'Ichiyo'** Double, shell-pink flowers with frilled edges in mid spring. Young foliage bronze-green. Upright habit. Relatively easy to find from specialist nurseries. **P. 'Imose'** Flowers double, mauve-pink, produced in hanging, loose clusters in mid spring. Young foliage copper-coloured, becoming bright green with good yellow autumn colour. Irregularly produces small, round, black fruits. Difficult to find. **P. 'Kanzan'** Very large clusters of double, purple-pink flowers produced in great profusion in mid spring. Young growth copper-red to red-brown, becoming dark green. Good autumn colours. Often confused with *P. 'Hisa-kura'* but they are distinct varieties, though similar in effect. **P. 'Ojochin'** Single flowers up to 2in (5cm) across in mid spring, pale pink in bud opening to pink-white in long hanging clusters of 7 or 8 florets. Young foliage bronze-brown becoming leathery and dark green with age. **P. 'Pink Perfection'** Pale pink flowers in mid to late spring. Rounded, fairly open habit. Young leaves bronze. Good yellow autumn tints. **P. 'Shimidsu Sakura'** syn. **P. serrulata var. longipes** Flowers double, pink in bud opening to pure white and hanging in clusters along the undersides of all branches in mid to late spring. Young foliage bright green, attractive. Good yellow autumn colours. Wide and spreading, forming a broad, flattened crown. **P. 'Shirofugen'** Flowers purple-pink in bud, aging through light pink to white. Foliage coppery when young, becoming light green. Good autumn tints. Forms a round-topped tree initially, spreading with age. **P. 'Shirotae'** syn. **P. 'Mount Fuji'** Single or semi-double flowers up to 2in (5cm) across, pure white and fragrant. Young

Prunus 'Tai Haku' in flower

Prunus 'Ukon'
in flower

**Average height
and spread**
Five years
12x8ft (3.5x2.5m)
Ten years
23x16ft (7x5m)
*Twenty years
or at maturity*
25x25ft (8x8m)

foliage light green; leaves have a distinctive fringed edge. Wide-spreading habit. Horizontal branches dipping sometimes to the ground. *P. 'Shosar'* Single, clear pink flowers in early to mid spring. Good orange-yellow autumn colours. Upright, pyramidal habit. *P. 'Tai Haku'* (Great White Cherry) Single, pure white flowers up to 2in (5cm) across, produced in great profusion in mid-spring. Young foliage copper-red. Spreading branches. Can be grown as large shrub or tree, and extremely attractive in both forms. *P. 'Taoyama Zakura'* Fragrant, semi-double, pale pink flowers in mid spring whitening with age. Good red-brown to copper-coloured young foliage. Low-growing with spreading habit. Relatively difficult to find in commercial production. *P. 'Ukon'* (Green Cherry) Hanging clusters of semi-double, pale green to green-yellow or cream flowers in mid spring, best seen against a background of clear blue sky. Interesting autumn foliage colours of red, yellow and orange.

PRUNUS SERRULATA VAR. PUBESCENS

KOREAN HILL CHERRY, ORIENTAL CHERRY
Rosaceae
Deciduous
Interesting dark autumn colour to foliage.

Origin From China, Korea and Japan.
Use For the unusual autumn foliage colouring.
Description *Flower* Small, single, pink flowers, produced in profusion in early spring.
Foliage Ovate, broad, up to 4in (10cm) long on younger wood, smaller on old. Dark green

giving way to beautiful deep purple or purple-red autumn colour. *Stem* Dark brown to mahogany brown. Twisted formation, rarely producing straight shoots. Forms a spreading domed tree with horizontal emphasis. Slow to medium growth rate. *Fruit* May produce tiny, uninteresting wine red fruits.
Hardiness Tolerates 4°F (−15°C).
Soil Requirements Most soil conditions, but poor soil produces poor growth.
Sun/Shade aspect Full sun to light shade. Sun enhances autumn colour; ideally seen against a blue sky.
Pruning None required.
Propagation and nursery production From budding or grafting on to understocks of *P. avium*. Plant bare-rooted or container-grown. Normally offered at 5-10ft (1.5-3m). Normally stocked by general and specialist nurseries.
Problems A twisted appearance is a natural characteristic of the tree's growth.

Prunus serrulata var. pubescens in autumn

Average height and spread
Five years
8x6ft (2.5x2m)
Ten years
16x13ft (5x4m)
Twenty years or at maturity
26x30ft (8x9m)

PRUNUS SUBHIRTELLA 'AUTUMNALIS'

WINTER-FLOWERING OR AUTUMN-FLOWERING CHERRY. HIGAN CHERRY
Rosaceae
Deciduous
Useful winter-flowering trees when mild weather allows.

Origin From Japan.
Use For autumn, winter or early spring flowering in most gardens. May also be considered as an attractive large shrub.
Description *Flower* Small white flowers, emerging on the bare branches in any mild weather period from late autumn to early spring. Flowering can be extensively delayed in cold winters, encouraging more vigorous spring blossoming. *Foliage* Small, ovate, up to 2in (5cm) long. Light green to grey-green. Good yellow autumn colours. *Stem* Wispy, branching, thin, grey-brown to grey-green, forming a round-topped, slightly spreading tree, or large shrub if grown without a central trunk. *Fruit* Insignificant.
Hardiness Tolerates 4°F (−15°C).
Soil Requirements Most soils; may show dis-

Prunus subhirtella
'Autumnalis Rosea'
in flower

tress on extremely poor types.

Sun/Shade aspect Tolerates light shade, but best seen in full light against a dark background.

Pruning None required.

Propagation and nursery production From budding or grafting on to understock of *P. avium*. Plant bare-rooted or container-grown. Offered in bush form without central trunk, or with stem of 5-6ft (1.5-2m) approximately. These are best planting heights, although larger trees may be available.

Problems Severe winter weather may kill some of the flowers, especially if they open before a cold spell. In wet, mild winters white varieties may be spotted pink by excessive rain. Young plants in nurseries rarely look substantial; trees take three or more seasons to establish and gain size.

Varieties of interest *P. s. 'Autumnalis Rosea'* Rosy pink flowers. *P. s. 'Fukubana'* Best grown as a large shrub, but in time can be encouraged to form a small tree. Produces semi-double, rose madder flowers in early spring.

Average height and spread

Five years
5x6ft (1.5x2m)
Ten years
16x13ft (5x4m)
Twenty years
or at maturity
24x24ft (7x7m)

PRUNUS Weeping Cherries

WEEPING CHERRY, JAPANESE CHERRY
Rosaceae
Deciduous
Truly aristocratic weeping trees, of exceptional spring beauty.

Origin From Japan. Mostly of garden or nursery origin.

Use As ornamental weeping trees, ideal for small, medium or large gardens. Best planted singly and isolated.

Description *Flower* Single or double, white or rose pink depending on variety, produced mid to late spring, often in profusion. *Foliage* Ovate, 5in (12cm) long, slightly tooth-edged. Light to mid green with some yellow autumn colour. *Stem* Weeping, pendulous stems to ground level, forming a circular, cascading fountain. Wood grey-brown and of winter interest. Medium rate of growth. *Fruit* Insignificant.

Hardiness Tolerates 4°F (−15°C).

Soil Requirements Most soil conditions, but resents poor soil.

Sun/Shade aspect Best in full sun. Tolerates limited light shade.

Pruning None required, but spread can be reduced by removal of outer weeping branches. Best carried out while tree is still dormant and wounds treated with pruning compound to prevent fungus disease.

Propagation and nursery production From grafting or budding on to understocks of *P. avium*. Plant bare-rooted or container-grown. Many varieties readily available, but some must be sought from specialist nurseries, including all forms of *P. subhirtella*. Normally supplied 5-8ft (1.5-2.5m) in height. Select a suitable shape and structure, allowing for increasing height once planted.

Prunus 'Kiku-shidare Sakura' **in flower**

Prunus × yedoensis
'Shidare Yoshino' in
flower

Problems Often planted in areas too small to accommodate it; may outgrow its location quite quickly. Must not be allowed to develop suckering growths, which may appear on main stem below grafted or budded point.

Varieties of interest *P. 'Hilling's Weeping'* Thin, slender, hanging branches, completely covered with a profusion of small white flowers in mid spring. Slightly less than average height and spread. *P. 'Kiku-shidare Sakura'* (Flowering Cherry) Large, double, pink flowers produced in mid to late spring, on the full length of the pendulous branches. Sometimes referred to as Cheal's Weeping Cherry. *P. subhirtella 'Pendula'* Thin, willow-like branches forming a low, spreading crown, with a profusion of small, off-white flowers in early to mid spring. One of the earliest to flower. *P. s. 'Pendula Rosea'* A rose pink flowering form, blossoming profusely in early spring. Height dependent on grafting. Average spread. *P. s. 'Pendula Rubra'* Dark pink to purple-pink flowers, very profuse in early spring. Height dependent on grafting. Average spread. *P. × yedoensis 'Ivensii'* Thin, hanging branches abundantly festooned with pure white flowers in mid spring. Extremely difficult to find in commercial production, and needs extensive search. *P. × yedoensis 'Shidare Yoshino'* syn. *P. × y. purpendens* (Yoshino Weeping Cherry of Japan) Vigorous, quick-growing, pendulous branches covered in mid spring with pink-budded flowers

Average height and spread
Five years
10x10ft (3x3m)
Ten years
13x16ft (4x5m)
Twenty years or at maturity
16x26ft (5x8m)

aging to pure white usually produced in short racemes. Slightly fragrant. Good yellow autumn colour. Readily available from specialist and general nurseries, but not normally stocked by garden centres.

PYRUS

ORNAMENTAL PEAR
Rosaceae
Deciduous
A range of trees with varying characteristics of merit for garden planting.

Origin From Europe through to Asia and Japan.
Use As a freestanding ornamental tree useful for any size of garden.
Description *Flower* Clusters up to 3in (8cm) across, composed of 5-7 white, single, cup-shaped florets, each up to 1½in (4cm) across, produced in mid spring. *Foliage* Ovate to linear, sometimes round. Green or silver-grey, depending on variety. Good autumn colours. *Stem* Grey-green to grey-brown. Upright, spreading or pendulous, depending on variety. Medium rate of growth in all cases. *Fruit* Small, oval or rounded pears up to 2in (5cm) long, in autumn. Fruits not edible.
Hardiness Tolerates −13°F (−25°C).
Soil Requirements Any soil type, but shows distress in extremely poor soils.
Sun/Shade aspect Green forms tolerate moderate shade. Silver-leaved varieties prefer full sun.
Pruning None required, but dead or crossing branches should be removed. May resent any other pruning.
Propagation and nursery production From grafting or budding on to understocks of pear, quince or *P. communis*. Available bare-rooted or container-grown. Normally offered

Pyrus calleryana 'Chanticleer' in flower

Pyrus salicifolia
'Pendula' in leaf

**Average height
and spread**
Five years
10x6ft (3x2m)
Ten years
16x13ft (5x4m)
*Twenty years
or at maturity*
26x20ft (8x6m)
72

from 4-10ft (1.2-3m) in height; occasionally available up to 13ft (4m). Best planting heights 5-8ft (1.5-2.5m). Most forms easily found in garden centres or general nurseries; some must be sought from specialist nurseries.

Problems All varieties are poor-rooted, especially when young. Extra peat or other organic material should be added to the planting hole to encourage establishment of young roots. Also needs extra watering in spring, and staking.

Varieties of interest *P. amygdaliformis* Foliage grey-green and ovate, white undersides. White flowers and insignificant fruits. Forms a round tree, becoming slightly pendulous with age. Rarely available. *P. calleryana 'Chanticleer'* Dark glossy green leaves maintained to late autumn and early winter, then turning orange-red. Narrow, columnar habit. Useful for all planting areas. *P. communis* (Wild Pear) Attractive white flowers in spring. Light green, ovate foliage with good autumn colour. Useful for windbreaks and exposed areas. Limited in commercial production; must be sought from specialist nurseries. *P. c. 'Beech Hill'* Dark green, round leaves; interesting leathery texture, glossy surface and wavy edges. Good autumn colours. Upright pyramidal habit. Useful for all gardens. *P. elaeagrifolia* Silver-grey ovate, sometimes lanceolate, foliage. Interesting white flowers. Slightly more tender than most but above average height. *P. nivalis* Attractive ovate, white to silver-grey foliage. Graceful white flowers. Small, globed, yellow-green fruits. Two-thirds average height and spread. Must be sought from specialist nurseries. *P. salicifolia 'Pendula'* (Weeping Willow-leaved Pear) Narrow, lanceolate leaves up to 2in (5cm) long. A round, mop-headed pendulous tree. Not usually as large as other forms when supplied. Attractive lawn specimen.

RHUS

SUMAC, SUMACH
Anacardiaceae
Deciduous
Small trees for autumn colours.

Origin From eastern North America.
Use As a freestanding tree or large shrub, planted singly or for inclusion in large shrub borders; or, if pruned hard, for mass planting.
Description *Flower* Flowers produced on wood two years old or more. Green panicles on male forms and dark pink on female forms; either or both forms may appear on a single plant. *Foliage* Large, pinnate leaves up to 18in (40cm) long and 6in (15cm) wide. Light to mid green, with edges of leaflets deeply toothed. Some lacerated and deeply cut. Very good rich autumn colours of yellow, red and orange. *Stem* Smooth or covered with red-brown hairs. Shoots upright when young, becoming branching, giving the effect of deer antlers. Forming a large, round-topped shrub which ultimately appears as a small, single or multi-stemmed 'tree'. Fast growing when young, slowing with age. *Fruit* Hairy plumes of scarlet fruits, produced in autumn and may be maintained into winter, eventually turning brown, on female plants only. Nurseries normally offer the female form, as fruits are a main characteristic of the plant.
Hardiness Tolerates −13°F (−25°C); in very severe conditions some stem damage may occur.
Soil Requirements Any soil type.
Sun/Shade aspect Full sun to light shade.
Pruning None required when grown as a tree. For maximum foliage effect, plants treated as shrubs can be cut to ground level and will rejuvenate with foliage three times the size of

Rhus typhina
in autumn

Average height and spread
Five years
6x6ft (2x2m)
Ten years
13x13ft (4x4m)
Twenty years or at maturity
20x20ft (6x6m)

that of unpruned plants. Unfortunately will not flower when grown under this practice, and reach less ultimate height.

Propagation and nursery production From root suckers freely produced. Planted bare-rooted or container-grown. *R. typhina* forms are relatively easy to obtain from most nursery outlets, but *R. glabra* forms may be more difficult to find. Best planting heights 2½-6ft (60cm-2m).

Problems Can be invasive, producing root suckers some distance from the parent plant. Young nursery plants always look gaunt and unattractive, but performance improves after planting out.

Varieties of interest *R. glabra* (Smooth Sumac) Slightly more than average spread. Smooth stems. Good autumn colour and good fruits in autumn. From eastern North America. *R. g. 'Laciniata'* Fern-like foliage, very deeply cut. Good orange, yellow and red autumn colours. May revert to non-lacerated form. *R. potaninii* Bright glossy green, pinnate foliage. Very shy to flower but may produce greenish white followed by red fruits. Difficult to find; try a specialist nursery. One-third more than average height and spread. From China. *R. trichocarpa* A large shrub or small tree with good orange-red autumn colour. Smooth stemmed. Yellow fruits. From China, Japan and Korea. *R. typhina* (Staghorn Sumac) Good autumn colours. Winter fruits in conical clusters, crimson aging to brown. Very free with root suckers. *R. t. 'Laciniata'* Very fine, deeply cut, pinnate foliage of fern-like appearance. Attractive shades of pastel orange and yellow in autumn.

ROBINIA Pink-flowering forms

FALSE ACACIA
Leguminosae
Deciduous
Attractive late spring-flowering trees, not well known and deserving more attention.

Origin South-western USA; some named varieties from France.

Use As large shrubs or small trees for flowering display. Ideal for all sizes of garden. Can be fan-trained on to a large wall if required, a procedure which shows off the flowers to best advantage.

Description *Flower* Clusters of pea-flowers, up to 3in (8cm) long on wood two years old or more, in early summer. *Foliage* Pinnate leaves, up to 6in (15cm) long with 9-11 oblong or ovate leaflets each 2in (5cm) long. Light grey-green with yellow autumn colours. *Stem* Light grey-green to grey-brown with small prickles. Upright when young, spreading and branching with age. Branches and twigs appear dead in winter, but produce leaves from apparently budless stems in late spring. Grown as large shrubs or as single-stemmed

Robinia kelseyi
in flower

trees. *Fruit* Small, grey-green, bristly pea-pods, up to 4in (10cm) long, in late summer and early autumn.

Hardiness Tolerates 14°F (−10°C) but stems may suffer some tip damage in severe winters.
Soil Requirements Most soil conditions; particularly tolerant of alkaline types. Resents waterlogging.
Sun/Shade aspect Full sun to very light shade.
Pruning None required. Young shoots can be shortened in early spring to encourage strong regrowth but this curtails flowering.
Propagation and nursery production From seed or grafting. Purchase container-grown. Normally available from 5-8ft (1.5-2.5m). Best planting heights 5-6ft (1.5-2m). Must be sought from general or specialist nurseries; most varieties not offered by garden centres.
Problems Notorious for poor establishment; container-grown trees provide best results. Branches may be damaged by high winds and need shelter.
Varieties of interest *R.* × *ambigua* Light pink flowers. Pinnate leaves with 13-21 light grey-green leaflets. Must be sought from specialist nurseries. *R.* *'Casque Rogue'* Rose-pink to pink-red flowers. An interesting variety from France. Difficult to find. *R. fertilis 'Monument'* Possibly best grown as a large suckering shrub, but can be encouraged to produce a single stem. Rosy red flowers. Half average height and spread. From south-eastern USA. *R.* × *hillieri* Slightly fragrant lilac-pink flowers. Originally raised in Hillier's Nurseries, Hampshire, England. *R. kelseyi* Flowers bright purple-pink. Attractive pale grey-

Average height and spread
Five years
10x6ft (3x2m)
Ten years
20x13ft (6x4m)
Twenty years or at maturity
39x20ft (12x6m)

75

green foliage with 9-11 leaflets. From south-eastern USA. Must be sought from specialist nurseries. *R. luxurians* Rose pink flowers. Leaves up to 12in (30cm) long, pinnate and with 15-25 oval bright green, leaflets. Slightly more than average height and spread. Not readily available; must be sought from specialist nurseries. From south-western USA.

ROBINIA PSEUDOACACIA 'FRISIA'

GOLDEN ACACIA
Leguminosae
Deciduous
An outstanding golden-foliaged tree.

Origin Of garden origin, from Europe.
Use As a freestanding tree or large shrub for most sizes of garden. Can also be fan-trained on a large wall.

Robinia pseudoacacia 'Frisia' **in leaf**

Description *Flower* Short racemes of white, pea-flowers, produced only on very mature trees in midsummer. *Foliage* Pinnate with 7-9 leaflets 6in (15cm) long. Bright yellow to yellow-green in spring, lightening in early summer. Turns deeper bright yellow in late summer to early autumn. *Stem* Brown to grey-brown. Strong shoots with definite red prickles on new growth. Wood may appear dead in winter but quickly grows away in late spring or early summer from apparently budless stems. An upright tree when young, becoming basal-spreading with age or can be grown as a large trunkless shrub. *Fruit* Insignificant.
Hardiness Tolerates 14°F (−10°C). Some stem-tip damage may occur in severe winters.
Soil Requirements Most soil conditions; growth is limited on very alkaline, permanently wet or poor soils. Grows best on moist, rich, loamy soil.

Sun/Shade aspect Full sun or very light shade. Deeper shade causes foliage to turn green.

Pruning None necessary, but shortening back side branches when young, on standards or bushes, encourages thicker, more attractive foliage and also controls size. Trees not fully established can benefit from the treatment, making new growth, and hence new roots.

Propagation and nursery production From grafting on to *R. pseudoacacia*. Purchase container-grown. Best planting heights 6-10ft (2-3m). Normally a single stem with very limited lateral branches is needed for a standard form. Single stem container-grown plants of 3ft (1m) can be used for fan-trained or bushy trees. Standard form readily available from most garden centres. Shorter bushes or trainable stock should be sought from general or specialist nurseries.

Problems Branches may be brittle and easily damaged by severe weather conditions. Late to break leaf, often bare until early summer, but grows rapidly once started. Notoriously difficult to establish unless container-grown.

Average height and spread
Five years
10x6ft (3x2m)
Ten years
20x13ft (6x4m)
Twenty years
or at maturity
39x20ft (12x6m)

ROBINIA PSEUDOACACIA
White-flowering varieties

ACACIA, BLACK LOCUST, FALSE ACACIA
Leguminosae
Deciduous
A stately tree, with several varieties of good shape and form.

Origin Native to the USA.

Use As a freestanding summer-flowering tree. Named varieties as featured specimen trees.

Description *Flower* Racemes of fragrant white flowers hanging in clusters up to 7in (17cm) long in early summer; florets have blotched yellow bases. Size can vary with age of tree and location. *Foliage* Pinnate, up to 10in (25cm) long, with 11-23 oval to ovate leaflets. Foliage light grey-green with good yellow autumn colour. *Stem* Grey-green to grey-brown and covered in thorns. Upright, quick-growing when young, slowing and branching with maturity. Appears completely dead in winter, but breaks leaf from almost budless stems. Produces suckers at ground level, often far from the central stem. *Fruit* Small, grey-green pea-pods up to 4in (10cm) long, in autumn.

Hardiness Tolerates 14°F (−10°C). Some stem-tip damage may occur in severe winters. High winds can cause physical damage to branches.

Soil Requirements Most soil conditions; dislikes waterlogging. Good on dry sandy soils.

Sun/Shade aspect Full sun to medium shade, preferring full sun.

Pruning None required, but may be reduced in size when young.

Propagation and nursery production From seed. Named varieties from grafting on to understocks of *R. pseudoacacia*. Best purchased container-grown or root-balled (balled-and-burlapped). Difficult to establish bare-rooted. Plants offered from 5-10ft (1.5-3m). Larger trees may be available but rarely transplant well. Stocked by general nurseries and specialist outlets.

Robinia pseudoacacia 'Bessoniana' in flower

Problems Subject to wind damage or mechanical breakage. Sometimes difficult to establish; extra organic or peat composts should be added to soil, and adequate watering supplied in first spring.

Varieties of interest *R. p. 'Bessoniana'* White flowers in early summer. The best white-flowering form for small gardens. Two-thirds average height and spread. *R. p. 'Inermis'* (Mop-head Acacia, Thornless Black Locust) Rarely flowers. Forms a tight, mop-headed tree 13x13ft (4x4m). Very slow-growing. Useful for all sizes of gardens for its interesting mature shape. Must be sought from specialist nurseries. *R. p. 'Pyramidalis'* syn. *R. p. 'Fastigiata'* Rarely flowers. Narrow, upright growth, slightly twisting branches. Forms an upright pillar of average height and maximum 6ft (2m) width. *R. p. 'Tortuosa'* Interesting contorted stems and bright green foliage, yellow autumn colour. Rarely flowers. Good architectural winter shape. Normally supplied at 3-5ft (1-1.5m). Useful for small gardens grown on a short trunk or as a bush. Two-thirds average height and spread.

Average height and spread
Five years
10x5ft (3x2.5m)
Ten years
26x16ft (8x5m)
Twenty years or at maturity
32x32ft (10x10m)
Continued growth over 50 years reaches 56x36ft (17x11m)

SORBUS AUCUPARIA

ROWAN, EUROPEAN MOUNTAIN ASH
Rosaceae
Deciduous
Well-known, attractive flowering and fruiting small trees.

Origin From Europe.
Use As small, attractive, ornamental trees suitable for all gardens, freestanding or grouped.
Description *Flower* Clusters of fluffy white flowers up to 5in (12cm) across produced in late spring, early summer. *Foliage* Pinnate, up to 9in (23cm) long with 11-15 leaflets, lanceolate with sharply toothed edges. Dark green with a slight grey sheen. Good orange-red or yellow autumn colours. *Stem* Green to green-brown, becoming grey-brown. Strong, upright when young, quickly spreading and eventually very branching. Mature wood has rubbery consistency. *Fruit* Clusters of red fruits in autumn, enjoyed by birds.
Hardiness Tolerates winter temperatures down to −13°F (−25°C).
Soil Requirements Most soil types, including very alkaline conditions.

Sorbus aucuparia
in fruit

**Average height
and spread**
Five years
8x5ft (2.5x1.5m)
Ten years
16x8ft (5x2.5m)
*Twenty years
or at maturity*
32x16ft (10x5m)
Continued growth
over 40 years
reaches 50x30ft
(15x9m)

*Sorbus aucuparia
'Beissneri' —*
branches

Sun/Shade aspect Best in full sun, but tolerates light shade.
Pruning None required.
Propagation and nursery production Parent
plant from seed; named forms by grafting or
budding on to understocks of *S. aucuparia*.
Available bare-rooted or container-grown.
Normally supplied from 3-10ft (1-3m); larger
plants occasionally available but best planting
heights 5-8ft (1.5-2.5m). Found in general
nurseries and garden centres.
Problems Birds take fruits readily in autumn.
S. aucuparia variable in size, flowering and
fruiting ability; unless mass planting is in-
tended named forms are more reliable.
Varieties of interest *S. a. 'Asplenifolia'* (Cut-
leaved Mountain Ash) Attractive deeply
toothed and dissected foliage, light green to
grey-green. White flowers and orange-red
fruits. *S. a. 'Beissneri'* (Orange-stemmed
Mountain Ash) Winter stems orange to
orange-red, a real attraction if planted in a
bright position. About two-thirds average
height and spread. *S. a. 'Fastigiata'* (Upright
Mountain Ash) Green foliage, white flowers
and dark red berries. Upright branches, forming a tall pillar. Susceptible to stem canker
and of weaker constitution than its parent. *S.
a. 'Pendula'* (Weeping Mountain Ash) White
flowers and red berries. A strong, ranging,
weeping tree reaching 10-13ft (3-4m) height
and 23-26ft (7-8m) spread. May suffer from
stem canker. *S. a. 'Sheerwater Seedling'*
Good, large foliage, white flowers and red
fruits in autumn. A good selected form of
upright growth. *S. a. 'Xanthocarpa'* (Yellow-
berried Mountain Ash) Yellow berries in
autumn. Light green foliage. Strong-growing

and attractive. *S. commixta* Large flowers, large red fruits, strong growth and good foliage. Uniform habit. A good selected form.

SORBUS Autumn foliage varieties

KNOWN BY BOTANICAL NAME
Rosaceae
Deciduous
Among the finest trees for autumn foliage colour.

Origin From Europe.
Use Freestanding or group planted to show off autumn tints.
Description *Flower* Clusters of fluffy white flowers, up to 5in (12cm) across in late spring, early summer. *Foliage* Pinnate, up to 9in (23cm) long with 11-15 lanceolate, sharply tooth-edged leaflets. Dark green with slight grey sheen. Excellent plum, orange and red autumn colours. *Stem* Green to green-brown, becoming grey-brown. Strong, upright when young, quickly becomes spreading and eventually very branching. *Fruit* Clusters of orange-red fruits in autumn, enjoyed by birds.

Sorbus 'Embley'
in autumn

Hardiness Tolerates −13°F (−25°C).
Soil Requirements Any soil type, including alkaline conditions.
Sun/Shade aspect Best in full sun, but tolerates light shade.
Pruning None required.
Propagation and nursery production By grafting or budding. Available bare-rooted or container-grown. Normally supplied from 3-10ft (1-3m), larger plants occasionally available. Heights of 5-8ft (1.5-2.5m) recommended as best for establishment. Readily found in general and specialist nurseries.
Problems None.
Varieties of interest *S. 'Embley'* syn. *S. discol-*

Average height
and spread
Five years
8x5ft (2.5x1.5m)
Ten years
16x8ft (5x2.5m)
Twenty years
or at maturity
32x16ft (10x5m)

81

Sorbus sargentiana in fruit

or Spectacular dark plum red autumn tints with some orange and yellow. Orange-red fruits not plentiful. *S. sargentiana* Spectacular orange to orange-red autumn colours. Large leaves. Stems light cream-green with red buds and thicker than most forms. Red to orange fruits. Normally available at only 3-6ft (1-2m) in height, upright when young becoming rounder with age.

SORBUS CASHMIRIANA

KASHMIR MOUNTAIN ASH
Rosaceae
Deciduous
One of the best autumn-fruiting trees.

Origin From Kashmir.
Use As a small tree or large shrub with attractive white autumn fruits planted singly or grouped.
Description *Flower* Hanging clusters of white flowers up to 5in (12cm) across in late spring, early summer. *Foliage* Pinnate, up to 9in (23cm) long with 9-11 leaflets. Grey-green with good yellow autumn colour. *Stem* Dark brown to brown-grey. Slow-growing short-branched and bushy nature. Forms a short round-topped tree or large shrub. *Fruit* Hanging clusters of pearl-white fruits in late summer or early autumn, maintained well into winter. Fruit stems red.
Hardiness Tolerates 4°F (−15°C).
Soil Requirements Any soil types.
Sun/Shade aspect Full sun to very light shade; fruits show well in autumn sunlight.
Pruning None required.
Propagation and nursery production From seed, grafting or budding. Available bare-rooted or container-grown. Normally offered from 3-6ft (1-2m). Relatively difficult to find; must be sought from specialist nurseries.

Average height and spread
Five years
6x6ft (2x2m)
Ten years
10x10ft (3x3m)
Twenty years or at maturity
13x13ft (4x4m)
82

Problems Moderate height and vigour should be taken into account when positioning, not overestimating space needed to accommodate ultimate height and spread.

Sorbus cashmiriana **in fruit**

SORBUS HUPEHENSIS

KNOWN BY BOTANICAL NAME

Rosaceae
Deciduous
A spectacular sight when fruiting in autumn.

Origin From China.
Use As a freestanding tree or particularly impressive for group planting.
Description *Flower* White flower clusters up to 4in (10cm) across in early summer. *Foliage* Grey-green with purple hue, up to 10in (25cm) long with 11-17 oblong leaflets, each 3in (8cm) long. *Stem* Purple-brown to dark brown. Upright when young, spreading slightly with age to form wide-topped tree. *Fruit* Hanging, open clusters of globe-shaped fruits, white tipped with pink.
Hardiness Tolerates winter temperatures down to −13°F (−25°C).
Soil Requirements Most soil conditions, but dislikes extremely alkaline types.
Sun/Shade aspect Full sun to light shade. Fruits show well in autumn sun.
Pruning None required.
Propagation and nursery production From grafting or budding on to understocks of *S. aucuparia*. Best purchased container-grown, but also available bare-rooted. Normally supplied at 5-10ft (1.5-3m). Larger trees occasionally available, but 5½-10ft (1.8-3m) best for establishment.
Problems None.
Varieties of interest *S. h. obtusa* Deep pink

Average height and spread
Five years
8x5ft (2.5x1.5m)
Ten years
16x8ft (5x2.5m)
Twenty years or at maturity
32x16ft (10x5m)

Sorbus hupehensis in fruit

fruits in autumn, otherwise similar to the parent.

SORBUS 'JOSEPH ROCK'

ROCK'S VARIETY
Rosaceae
Deciduous
On the right soil, one of the finest yellow-fruiting autumn trees.

Origin Of garden origin.
Use As a freestanding specimen tree planted singly or grouped; or sited in a large shrub border as an autumn attraction.
Description *Flower* White flower clusters in mid spring to early summer. *Foliage* Pinnate leaves, up to 6in (15cm) long with 9-11 leaflets. Some yellow-orange autumn tints. Mature foliage can be a little disappointing in both summer and autumn. *Stem* Grey-green, becoming grey-brown. Pyramidal, becoming ascending at maturity, forming a tight, neat small tree of medium vigour. *Fruit* Hanging clusters of yellow to yellow-orange fruits, profuse and well displayed in autumn.
Hardiness Tolerates 4°F (−15°C).
Soil Requirements Tolerates most soil conditions, but requires rich, deep loam to show best foliage and fruiting ability. Rapidly becomes old and stunted on poor soils.
Sun/Shade aspect Full sun. Autumn and winter sun show fruits to best advantage.
Pruning None required.
Propagation and nursery production From grafting or budding on to *S. aucuparia*. Nor-

Average height and spread
Five years
8x5ft (2.5x1.5m)
Ten years
16x8ft (5x2.5m)
Twenty years or at maturity
32x16ft (10x5m)

84

mally available bare-rooted or container-grown from 5½-10ft (1.8-3m). Larger trees may be available, but smaller more likely to succeed. Readily found in garden centres and general nurseries.

Problems Cannot do well on poor soil conditions. Often sells out due to its wide popularity; early ordering from nurseries may be advisable.

Sorbus 'Joseph Rock' in fruit

STUARTIA PSEUDOCAMELLIA
(Stewartia pseudocamellia)

KNOWN BY BOTANICAL NAME

Theaceae
Deciduous
An acid-loving large shrub or small tree, with good flowers and beautiful autumn colours.

Origin From Japan.
Use As a large, freestanding shrub or small tree for gardens, or as a small arboretum specimen.
Description *Flower* Cup-shaped, pure white flowers up to 2in (5cm) across, in mid to late

85

summer. Petals incurved with jagged margins and very silky texture. Stamens white with pronounced orange-yellow anthers. Trees take 5-10 years to come into full flowering. *Foliage* Ovate, slightly tooth-edged, 4in (10cm) long. Grey-green giving good orange-red autumn colours. *Stem* Young shoots grey-green. Quick-growing once established. Stems aging to brown-grey, often with red-orange sheen in spring. Forms a slow-growing large pyramidal shrub, ultimately tree-forming. *Fruit* Insignificant.

Hardiness Tolerates 14°F (−10°C).

Soil Requirements Requires an acid soil, moist, rich and deep for good growth. Dislikes any alkalinity.

Sun/Shade aspect Best in light shade. Tolerates full sun but may suffer leaf scorch in summer.

Stuartia pseudocamellia in flower

Pruning Rarely required.

Propagation and nursery production From seed or layers. Purchase container-grown. Normally supplied between 2ft (60cm) and 3ft (1m), the best heights for planting. Must be sought from specialist nurseries.

Problems Must have acid soil. Vulnerable to sun scorch.

Varieties of interest *S. koreana* Broader foliage than *S. pseudocamellia* and larger flowers. Difficult to obtain; must be sought from specialist nurseries. From Korea. *S. malacodendron* Foliage up to 4in (10cm) long, ovate or oval, with good autumn colours. Pure white flowers 3in (8cm) across, violet anthers and white stamens. One-third average height and spread. Normally considered a large shrub. From south-eastern USA and extremely rare outside its native environment. *S. sinensis* Interesting peeling, dull, orange-brown bark over a grey undersurface. Foliage oval to oblong, up to 4in (10cm) long, slightly tooth-edged, bright green with good orange-yellow autumn colours. White fragrant flowers up to 2in (5cm) across, with yellow anthers. Two-thirds average height and spread. From China. Difficult to obtain. Other *Stuartia* varieties are offered, but those listed are best for general garden use.

Average height and spread

Five years
5x3ft (1.5x1m)
Ten years
13x6ft (4x2m)
Twenty years or at maturity
32x16ft (10x5m)

SYRINGA Cultivars

LILAC, STANDARD LILAC
Oleaceae
Deciduous
Attractive spring-flowering 'toy' trees, trained from the so-called Standard Lilac commonly grown as a shrub.

Origin Of garden origin; many raised by Victor Lemoine and his son, Émile, in their nursery in Nancy, France. Varieties may show only slight differences of size or colour.
Use As small specimen trees for spot planting and to emphasize garden features.
Description *Flower* Single or double florets in large, fragrant panicles, late spring or early summer. Colour range blue to lilac, pink to red or purple; also white, yellow, and some bicoloured forms. Colour, size and flowering time dependent on variety. *Foliage* Medium-sized, ovate leaves, dark green to mid green. *Stem* Grey-green to grey-brown. Stout shoots with pronounced buds, yellow or red-purple in winter, dependent on variety. Standard forms pretrained from ground level; or by budding or grafting at 5-8ft (1.5-2.5m) on single stems. Round, single-stemmed, mop-headed or slightly pyramidal trees. *Fruit* Grey-brown seedheads of some winter attraction.
Hardiness Tolerates winter temperatures down to −13°F (−25°C).
Soil Requirements Most soil conditions, but may show signs of chlorosis on severe alkaline types.
Sun/Shade aspect Full sun to medium shade, preferring full sun.
Pruning Very little required but removal of seedheads in winter encourages flower production. Can be drastically cut back to control vigour but this leads to reduced flowering in the next 2-3 years.
Propagation and nursery production From budding and grafting using *S. vulgaris* or the common Privet, *Ligustrum vulgare* or *L. ovalifolium* as understock. Can also be raised

Syringa 'Monique Lemoine' in flower

**Average height
and spread**
Five years
7x3ft (2.2x1m)
Ten years
12x5ft (3.5x1.5m)
*Twenty years
or at maturity*
16x8ft (5x2.5m)

from semi-ripe cuttings taken early to mid summer. Single, individual shoots are trained from ground level; budding or grafting takes place at 3-5ft (1-1.5m) from ground level on pretrained understock. Available bare-rooted or container-grown. Standard forms grown as mop-headed trees are relatively scarce in production.

Problems Top growth of standard forms somewhat weak and very susceptible to wind damage; requires good staking.

Varieties of interest *S. 'Charles Joly'* Double, dark red-purple flowers in large panicles produced late spring to early summer. *S. 'Katherine Havemeyer'* Large, broad, bold lavender-blue flowers. Strong, rounded, bright green foliage. *S. 'Monique Lemoine'* syn. *S. 'Madame Lemoine'* Large, pure white double flowers produced in mid spring. *S. 'Souvenir de Louis Spaeth'* Single wine red flowers in broad trusses produced in mid to late spring. Strong-growing.

Many varieties can be grown as standards. Those listed are most suitable for garden plants and available commercially.

WISTERIA Standard trees

WISTERIA, STANDARD WISTERIA

Leguminosae
Deciduous
Interesting training of a normally climbing plant to form a spreading, weeping tree.

Origin Mostly from China.

Use As a spreading, weeping, mop-headed, small tree. Best grown as a single lawn specimen in medium-sized or larger gardens.

Description *Flower* Racemes of blue, white or pink flowers, depending on variety, up to 12in (30cm) long, produced in late spring and cascading in a long waterfall effect. *Foliage* Pinnate and consisting of 11 oval to oblong leaflets, each leaf up to 12in (30cm) long, light green in colour with some yellow autumn tints. *Stem* Single, upright stem encourage. Grey-green quickly becoming grey-brown, old and gnarled. Requires support throughout its life. After 10-20 years forms a widely spread, arched and weeping effect. *Fruit* Grey-green pea-pods in autumn.

Hardiness Tolerates 4°F (−15°C).

Soil Requirements Most soil conditions, but dislikes extreme alkalinity.

Sun/Shade aspect Best in light dappled shade, but tolerates full sun.

Pruning Tendrils from new summer growth cut back hard in early autumn to two buds to encourage central crown of mainly flowering wood. Mop-headed effect formed by shortening tendrils by one-third.

Propagation and nursery production From grafting of named varieties on to *W. sinensis*, then encouraging a central, single trunk and short cut-back head. Normally supplied from 6-8ft (2-2.5m). Not readily available and must be sought from specialist nurseries. Garden training is by selecting a single stem and encouraging it as sole wood producer by staking and removing all unrequired tendrils. Head may be trained on to wire umbrella support.

Problems Trees may take between 5-10 years to come into flower. Can be somewhat unruly and misshapen, and require extensive annual pruning.

Varieties of interest *W. sinensis* Blue, hanging flowers up to 12in (30cm) long. Only use grafted plants from a good known source: seed-raised trees are unreliable. *W. s. 'Alba'* White racemes of flowers up to 10in (25cm)

Wisteria sinensis in flower

Average height and spread
Five years
10x6ft (3x2m)
Ten years
13x13ft (4x4m)
Twenty years or at maturity
16x20ft (5x6m)

long. *W. s. 'Rosea'* Pink to rose pink, hanging flower racemes 10in (25cm) long.

Any *Wisteria* variety can be trained in this way. The above are selected from the range of flower colours.

PLANTING TREES

Successful establishment of a tree begins with the important stage of preparing a correctly sized planting hole. The planting process may seem somewhat laborious, but it is worthwhile providing the best conditions in which the plant can grow and thrive rather than merely survive, as it may be the focal point of the garden and can give years of pleasure if allowed to establish itself properly.

Any perennial weed roots, such as couch grass, dock or thistles, must be cleared from the site, otherwise they become almost impossible to remove and grow strongly in competition. If the planting area is grass-covered, turves should be removed before preparation of the planting hole. If free from weeds, they may later be replaced upside down to conserve moisture in the turned-over soil after planting.

Preparing the planting hole
The diameter and depth of the planting area depends upon the size of tree, as follows:

For trees up to 9ft (2.8m) when purchased, the planting hole should be 3ft (1m) in diameter. For larger trees, up to 16ft (5m), the required size of planting hole is 4½ft (1.4m) or more.

The depth of preparation is the same for trees of all heights – 18in (50cm). The soil is worked over in two stages: planting depth corresponds to the original depth of soil around the tree or shrub, whether it is supplied bare-rooted or root-balled (balled-and-burlapped) or has been grown in a container, but a similar depth of soil is broken up and prepared below the actual planting depth.

Remove the topsoil to a depth of 9in (25cm). Store the soil on a flat board beside the planting hole and add to it half a bucket of compost or well-rotted farmyard manure.

Fork over and break up a further 9in (25cm) of subsoil. Remove any weed roots from the soil as it is turned. Dig in half a bucket of compost or well-rotted farmyard manure.

Planting a container-grown tree
A container-grown tree should be well-watered before it is planted, ideally at least one hour beforehand.

Place the plant, still in its container, in the planting hole and adjust the depth so the rim of the container is just below the surrounding soil level. If the tree is in a rigid or flexible plastic container, this can now be removed, taking care not to disturb the soil ball around the roots of the plant. (A young tree will need staking at this point – see below.) Peat composition or treated paper pots can be left in place as the material is decomposable except in very dry conditions.

Never lift the plant by its trunk or stems,

as this can tear and damage the roots. Handle the whole root ball carefully and once the container has been removed, take care that small exposed roots do not dry out.

Replace the prepared topsoil around the root ball of the plant to the level of the soil around the planting hole. Tread the soil gently all around the plant to compress it evenly. Unless the soil is very wet, pour a bucket of water into the depressed area.

Fill the area with more prepared topsoil; bringing the level up just above that of the surrounding soil. Dig a small V-shaped trench, 3in (8cm) deep and wide, around the planting area to allow drainage.

Planting a bare-rooted tree
The basic planting method is the same for bare-rooted or root-balled (balled-and-burlapped) plants as for container-grown, but it is even more important that the roots should not be allowed to dry out. When returning the topsoil to the planting hole, take care to work it well in around the roots of the tree or shrub, leaving no air pockets in the soil.

Staking a tree
A young tree should be staked as soon as it is placed in the planting hole. The stake should be at least 1-1½in (3-4cm) thick, round or square-sectioned with a pointed tip, and treated to resist rotting. Select a suitable length to support the height and weight of the tree – the top of the stake should extend well into the upper stems or branches, and the point should go into the subsoil to a

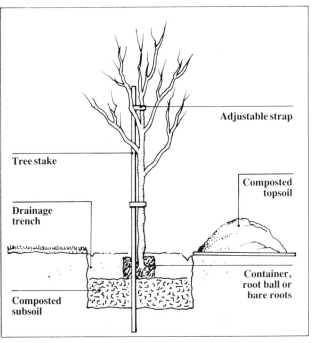

Adjustable strap

Tree stake

Composted topsoil

Drainage trench

Container, root ball or bare roots

Composted subsoil

depth of 18in (50cm).

When the tree is in place in the planting hole, push the stake through the soil ball and into the prepared subsoil below. If it meets a definite obstruction, remove the stake and try in a different spot, but not more than 2in (5cm) from the tree stem.

To support the tree, fasten two adjustable ties, with small spacing blocks to hold the tree clear of the stake, one on the stem among the branches as high as is practical, the other halfway up the main stem or trunk. From time to time as the tree grows, check the ties and loosen them as necessary so they do not restrict the trunk.

Watering and feeding

The danger period for loss of any plant is in the spring and summer following planting. In dry conditions, water the tree well at least three times a week.

If the tree or shrub is planted in spring, early or late in the season, apply one gloved handful of bonemeal. If planting is carried out in any other season, apply the bonemeal early in the spring following planting, and repeat annually thereafter. A general purpose liquid fertilizer can also be given annually in midsummer.

Planting times – UK and Europe

Bare-rooted or root-balled trees can be planted at any time from late autumn to early spring, except in the harshest of winter conditions. Do not plant when the ground is frozen or waterlogged.

Container-grown trees can be planted at any time of year, unless weather conditions are extreme. Do not plant when the ground is frozen, dried hard, or waterlogged.

Planting times – USA

The best time to plant bare-rooted trees is in late winter or early spring, just before bud break. Bare-rooted trees lose most of their root surface – and water-absorbing capacity – during transplanting. New roots will not develop until spring, so if you plant in fall, there is the risk that buds and twigs will dry out over winter.

Fall is the best time to plant balled-and-burlapped and container-grown trees, because it gives them a long season of cool air and warm soil for strong root growth. Roots put on most of their year's growth after leaf-fall.

Planting times – Australia and New Zealand

Bare-rooted or root-balled trees can be planted at any time from late autumn to early spring, unless the ground is frozen hard or waterlogged.

Container-grown trees and shrubs can be planted at any time of year unless weather conditions are extreme. Do not plant when the ground is frozen, dried hard or water-logged. It is advisable to avoid planting in midsummer when conditions are extremely hot and dry.

PRUNING

Correct pruning of a tree can improve and increase the plant's flowering and fruiting, the size and colour of foliage, and the appearance of attractive stems and bark. Most importantly for the gardener, it controls and shapes the growth of the tree, so that it remains an attractive garden feature suited to the location where it is growing.

Specific pruning instructions for individual trees are given in the text entries. In some cases it is not necessary to prune, but all trees should be inspected every spring for broken twigs and branches and other signs of damaged wood, which is not only unsightly but also vulnerable to disease. Soft or woody growth which has suffered winter die-back should also be cut back in spring. Trees frequently develop crossing branches which may rub together and cause a lesion that may become the site of various diseases. The weaker of the two branches should be removed in winter, or while the plant is dormant, and this is also the best time to check for signs of fungus disease, as fungus spores are inactive in winter and if the damaged area is removed there is little chance that the disease will spread.

Methods of pruning
Many trees require no pruning unless growth has to be confined in a restricted space, while others actively resent pruning and if cut will tend to die back. It may also be inadvisable to prune if this will remove flower buds at the terminals of twigs or branches. Otherwise, a plant can be lightly trimmed or pruned back hard, or growth may be selectively removed to encourage new growth production.

Pollarding is a system of pruning applied to some trees, in which all growth produced in the previous year is cut back in late winter or early spring to form a crown of old growth from which the new spring display emerges vigorously. It is also possible to cease pruning for two to three years to allow the tree to increase in size, resuming the pollarding process again when the tree becomes too large or its features are losing some of their interest.

You can distinguish between one- or two-year-old wood and old or mature wood by colour and texture. One-year-old wood is new growth produced between the spring and autumn of the same year, light in colour and relatively flexible with a soft texture. Two-year-old wood is the previous season's growth, usually darker and stiffer with the beginnings of a bark. Old or mature wood is shown by thick stems, dark colour and noticeably tougher bark texture.

Pruning cuts
It is important to cut a stem at the correct angle when pruning, at a point slightly above a bud with the cut sloping away from it at a gentle angle (below).

INDEX OF LATIN NAMES

INDEX OF COMMON NAMES